Paul on the Mystery of Israel

Daniel J. Harrington, S.J.

A Michael Glazier Book
THE LITURGICAL PRESS
Collegeville, Minnesota

Zacchaeus Studies: New Testament

General Editor: Mary Ann Getty

A Michael Glazier Book published by The Liturgical Press

Cover design by David Manahan, O.S.B.

Cover illustration: Detail of mosaic "Paul at Damascus," Palatine
      Chapel, Palermo.

1   2   3   4   5   6   7   8   9

Library of Congress Cataloging-in-Publication Data

Harrington, Daniel J.
      Paul on the mystery of Israel / Daniel J. Harrington.
          p.   cm. — (Zacchaeus studies.   New Testament)
      "A Michael Glazier book."
      Includes bibliographical references and indexes.
      ISBN 0-8146-5035-X
      1. Paul, the Apostle, Saint—Views on Jews and Judaism.   2. Bible.
N.T.   Romans XI, 25–32—Commentaries.   3. Paul, the Apostle,
Saint.   I. Title.   II. Series.
BS2655.J4H375   1992
227'.106—dc20   92-18312
                                                                       CIP

Contents

Editor's Note

Zacchaeus Studies provide concise, readable and relatively inexpensive scholarly studies on particular aspects of scripture and theology. The New Testament section of the series presents studies dealing with focal or debated questions; and the volumes focus on specific texts or particular themes of current interest in biblical interpretation. Specialists have their professional journals and other forums where they discuss matters of mutual concern, exchange ideas and further contemporary trends of research; and some of their work on contemporary biblical research is now made accessible for students and others in *Zacchaeus Studies*.

The authors in this series share their own scholarship in nontechnical language, in the areas of their expertise and interest. These writers stand with the best in current biblical scholarship in the English-speaking world. Since most of them are teachers, they are accustomed to presenting difficult material in comprehensible form without compromising a high level of critical judgment and analysis.

The works of this series are ecumenical in content and purpose and cross credal boundaries. They are designed to augment formal and informal biblical study and discussion. Hopefully they will also serve as texts to enhance and supplement seminary, university and college classes. The series will also aid Bible study groups, adult education and parish religious education classes to develop intelligent, versatile and challenging programs for those they serve.

Mary Ann Getty
New Testament Editor

Introduction

Making a statement about the Catholic Church's relationship to the Jewish people was very high on Pope John XXIII's agenda when he called the Second Vatican Council. The statement had a complicated history during the Council. But it finally appeared as section 4 in "The Declaration of the Relationship of the Church to Non-Christian Religions," commonly known by its first two Latin words *Nostra aetate* ("in our age").

The conciliar statement acknowledges the Church's spiritual debt to the people of Israel, affirms Israel's spiritual privileges and calls them irrevocable, expresses a hope for greater spiritual unity in the future, encourages cooperation in the present, denies that all Jews bear responsibility for Jesus' death, stresses the importance of inculcating proper attitudes toward Jews and Judaism through catechesis and preaching, and rejects persecutions and displays of anti-Semitism. The full text of *Nostra aetate* 4 is provided in the appendix to this book.

The results of the conciliar statement over the past twenty-five or so years have been quite positive. There surely have been high and low points in the new relationship. The old attitudes die hard in some quarters, and even the best intentions easily get caught up in the bitter memories of the Holocaust and the complications of Middle Eastern politics. But it is fair to say that the Church's new relationship with the Jewish people outlined in *Nostra aetate* 4 has been one of the great successes of Vatican II. One prominent Jewish leader has called the new relationship irreversible, and a distinguished Protestant theologian has stated that now the Church can no longer be "within" or "against" Judaism (as it has been) but rather must be "with" the Jewish people.

One of the Council's recommendations was that Christians and Jews examine their common spiritual heritage. It went on to suggest: "This can be obtained, especially, by way of biblical and theological enquiry and through friendly discussions." Since the Council, there have been many (usually friendly) discussions among Christians and Jews. There has also been a revival of interest in certain biblical and theological issues that, for many years, lay dormant. These issues include the place of the "Old Testament" in Christian life, the nature of God's covenant relationship(s) with Israel and the Church, the Jewishness of Jesus, the historical responsibility for Jesus' death, Jesus' attitude toward the Torah, Paul's attitude toward Judaism, when and how Israel and the Church came to a parting of the ways, and whether it is proper to call the New Testament or any part of it anti-Semitic. These questions have been addressed by both Jews and Christians. And great progress has been made, often times simply by listening to the conflicting positions and trying to sort out what can and cannot be held. Of course, there are other issues—historical, theological, and political—that divide Christians and Jews. Nevertheless, the issues that pertain to the Bible are important.

When reading the text of *Nostra aetate* 4, anyone familiar with the Bible will immediately recognize the overwhelming influence of Paul's writings. Not only are there several explicit quotations from Paul's letters, but much of the statement reads as something of a paraphrase of Paul. Those who wrote the conciliar statement clearly thought that Paul had some important and positive things to say about the Church's relationship to the Jewish people.

There is a certain irony in the Council's reliance on Paul to build a new relationship with the Jewish people. Many Jews (and some Christians) regard Paul as the one who was responsible for dividing Christians and Jews in the first place. They contend that, without Paul, the Church would have remained a sect within Judaism. They blame Paul for providing the language and theology that led not only to the parting of the ways, but also to negative attitudes toward Jews that saw a hideous climax in the Holocaust.

Is Paul the friend or the enemy of the Jewish people? Are Paul's writings the basis for a new and positive relationship between Christians and Jews, or a reason for a 2,000-year history of hatred and suffering? These are serious questions.

Paul's attitude toward Jews and Judaism is a "hot" topic in biblical studies today. An enormous bibliography has developed to which both Christians and Jews have contributed. There are charges of revisionism, trendiness, heresy, and conservatism. The claims and counterclaims about what Paul really thought regarding the Jewish people and the Torah in the light of the Christ-event are sometimes bewildering.

When the *Zacchaeus Studies* series was inaugurated about six years ago, I volunteered to be among the first batch of writers. I wanted to write a little book on "Paul and Judaism," with particular attention to the "mystery of Israel" outlined in Romans 11:25-26. I thought the writing would be easy. I had followed the scholarly debates for years. I had studied the pertinent texts and lectured on them many times. And *Zacchaeus Studies* seemed to be the appropriate vehicle, since I wanted to lead non-specialists through the major texts and introduce them to the issues debated by scholars.

As I first began my work on the book, I realized how confused the scholarship was on Paul and Judaism, and how confused I was by it. Confused authors write confusing books. So I abandoned the project for awhile. But I continued to lecture on the texts and to read the scholarship. And finally, after six years, I think that I have reached the intellectual clarity that allows me to offer a book on Paul and Judaism for *Zacchaeus Studies*. The topic is still lively, and I think that I now know what I am talking about.

This book takes its title *Paul on the Mystery of Israel* from what Paul wrote in Romans 11:25-26: "I want you to understand this mystery: a hardening has come upon part of Israel, until the full number of Gentiles has come in. And so all Israel will be saved." The mystery for Paul was the rejection of the gospel by (a large) part of Israel and what God planned for Israel in the future. The aim of the book is to lead the reader through the Pauline texts that relate to Paul's statement on the mystery of Israel and to provide a guide to the principal scholarly issues and debates that enrich our appreciation of the texts and their theological content.

The plan of the book follows from its aim. The first chapter places Paul's statements on the mystery of Israel in the context of Paul's letters, his life as a Jew, and his theology. The second chapter examines Paul's comments on Jews and Jewish Christians as they appear in 1 Thessalonians 2:14-16, Galatians, 2 Corinthians 3, and Philippians 3. The third chapter considers what Paul said in various parts of his letter to the Romans, especially in chapters 2-3 and 9-11. The fourth chapter is a detailed exposition of the focal text of the study: Romans 11:25-32. The fifth chapter examines five issues that are debated among modern scholars: Paul the convert, his apostleship to the Gentiles, his attitude toward the Law, the tensions within his attitude, and the future of Israel ("and so all Israel will be saved"). The final chapter draws some theological conclusions from the exegesis and scholarly debates. The appendix provides the text of *Nostra aetate* 4, since the Pauline influence on it is so great and since it provides the occasion for rethinking in an orderly way what Paul said about Jews and Judaism.

All biblical quotations are from the New Revised Standard Version. I have made one modification: In texts where "law" clearly refers to the Mosaic Law, I have capitalized the word in the interest of clarity.

The list of suggested readings is longer than is customary in *Zacchaeus Studies*. This is so because so much has been written on the topic and because this book is intended to encourage readers to go further into the research of the topic. I have marked what I regard as the most important books with an asterisk.

As I have already explained, this little book has a long history. I must thank Michael Glazier, Mary Ann Getty, and Michael Naughton, O.S.B. for their patience and encouragement. And I thank especially my students at Weston School of Theology for their interest in and critical approach to the topic. It must be disturbing to hear a professor state at the beginning of a course: "I don't know what I think about this topic." I hope that they learned as much as I did. I thank them for helping me to know what I think about Paul on the mystery of Israel.

1

Paul in Context

Paul is justly regarded as one of the great theologians in the Christian tradition. Yet this assessment might have puzzled Paul himself. Paul was not a professional writer or a teacher in the formal sense. Rather, he was an apostle, commissioned to preach the good news of Jesus Christ and to found Christian communities. His writings were only an extension of his apostleship, one part of his strategy to help other early Christians to live out their new faith.

It is important to read Paul on his own terms, in his historical context, if we wish to know what he held about Jews and Judaism. Paul's statements on these matters were made in letters addressed mainly to Gentile Christians by a Diaspora Jew. Gentile Christians were struggling to understand their identity vis-à-vis Jewish Christians and other Jews. In his efforts to help these Gentiles, Paul was surely straining the boundaries of Judaism as it was understood in his day. Paul's experience of Christ had made everything else—even matters such as circumcision and the Law—relatively unimportant. In his own context, Paul was a pioneering pastoral theologian.

Paul's Letters

Within the canon of New Testament books, Paul is a major figure. Of the twenty-seven documents in the canon, thirteen letters are ascribed to Paul, Acts makes Paul one of its heroes, and Hebrews has some connection with Paul. This study of Paul on the mystery of Israel, however, will focus on the seven undisputed Pauline letters: 1 Thessalonians, Galatians, 1–2 Corinthians, Philippians, Philemon, and Romans. There is no serious doubt that Paul wrote these letters, and so Paul's own words on the topic of Israel will be the focus of attention.

Paul wrote these seven letters in the "fifties" of the first century A.D. They are the writings not of a systematic theologian or a professor, but rather of a pastoral theologian. The letters are substitutes for Paul's personal presence and respond to issues that had arisen in his absence. Except in the case of Romans, Paul had introduced the people whom he addressed to Christianity. As Paul continued his missionary travels, word got back to him of certain problems and abuses. His letters were intended to bring the light of Christian faith to the difficulties experienced by the early Christians.

Paul was no lonely genius. Rather, his major task was founding and building up Churches in present-day Turkey and Greece. He even hoped to extend his mission as far as Spain (see Rom 15:24). In carrying out his missionary task, Paul developed and relied upon a network of helpers and of communication (see Rom 16:1-16). His letters were one facet in this network. And most of them (Romans and Galatians are exceptions) are presented as joint compositions (with Timothy, Sosthenes, etc.).

One of the major pastoral problems that Paul faced among his new Christians was their identity with respect to the people of Israel and the practices of Judaism. Paul did not invent the mission to the Gentiles (see Acts 10-11). But he did become its major proponent and practitioner. He was willing to admit non-Jews (Gentiles, or pagans) into the Christian community without forcing them to be circumcised or placing upon them the obligations of the OT Law (Torah). In other words, Gentiles did not have to become Jews in order to become Christians.

What was clear to Paul and his Gentile converts was not acceptable to all early Christians. On the one hand, some Jewish Christians regarded Paul's circumcision-free and Law-free gospel to be a truncated and inadequate version of Christian faith. They looked upon their movement as remaining within Judaism, as a particular manifestation of Judaism, and so they expected that Gentiles who became Christians would also become Jews. And thus, such Jewish Christians sought to undo or at least correct Paul's gospel by mounting some kind of missionary campaign. This Jewish-Christian "corrective" campaign forms the background of Paul's comments in Galatians, Philippians, and 2 Corinthians.

On the other hand, some Gentile Christians seem to have been fascinated by Judaism. On becoming Christians, they may well have wanted to go further into Judaism. Judaism was attractive to many people in the Greco-Roman world.[1] Its attractions included a lively sense of community, high ethical standards, and faith in one God. And since Jesus whom the Gentile Christians confessed as "Lord" was a Jew, and Paul, who brought them the gospel, was a Jew, and their movement was generally regarded as a Jewish movement, it was only natural that such Gentiles would be impressed by the claims of Jewish Christians that full Christianity involved circumcision and Torah observances.

The Church at Rome offered another variant of the problem of Christian identity with respect to Judaism. Christianity arose in Rome very early (in the thirties or forties) in the large Jewish community there. Before the Jews were expelled by the emperor Claudius in A.D. 49 (see Acts 18:2), there were both Jewish and Gentile Christians at Rome. When the Jews were allowed back to Rome in A.D. 54, relations between the two groups were naturally strained. In the absence of the Jewish Christians, the Gentiles had dominated Church life in Rome. When the Jewish Christians returned, they assumed that dominance would naturally revert to them. They were mistaken. And so Paul wrote to the Romans to explain how both Jews and Gentiles could live as part of the one body of Christ.

The issue of Gentile-Christian identity vis-à-vis Jewish Christianity and Judaism was among the most pressing matters that Paul the pastoral theologian treated in his seven undisputed letters. Paul sought to explain to Gentiles why they did not have to take up circumcision and Torah observances to become per-

---

[1]L. H. Feldman, "Proselytes and 'Sympathizers' in the Light of the New Inscriptions from Aphrodisias," *Revue des Etudes Juives* 148 (1989) 265–305.

fect Christians. He tried to make clear to Jewish Christians that they should not impose their kind of Christianity upon Gentiles. He wanted both Christian groups to live in harmony and mutual respect.

Through the medium of his letters, Paul continued to serve as a pastor. He dealt with the problems facing real people in the mid-first century as they struggled to understand their identity as Christians. Paul carried out his pastoral task, however, as a theologian also. He appealed to authoritative formulas of faith (see Rom 1:3-4; 1 Cor 15:3-5; Phil 2:6-11; etc.) and the Scriptures. He reflected on the implications of Jesus' death and resurrection. He drew consequences for Christian action and resolved disputes on theological principles. Paul's letters are the work of a pastoral theologian.

Paul the Jew

The Judaism into which Paul was born was both diverse and international. These two characteristics of first-century Judaism were very significant for the development of early Christianity.

Recognition of first-century Judaism's diversity was helped by the discovery of the Dead Sea Scrolls in the late 1940's. Whereas scholars had routinely divided Jews and Jewish writings between Pharisees and Sadducees, the Dead Sea scrolls provided evidence for at least one other branch of Judaism (most likely Essenism). They also led scholars to rethink the sociological map of Judaism in Jesus' time. There were a few constants: the Temple, the land, and the Law. But even with these constants, there were debates about significance and interpretation. Restudy of the Old Testament Pseudepigrapha, the Targums, the Septuagint, and the rabbinic writings have revealed a rich diversity within Judaism.

The change in perception can be illustrated by two book titles. Thirty-five years ago, Joseph Klausner's study of Jewish messianism was entitled *The Messianic Idea in Israel*, and Sigmund Mowinckel's *He That Cometh* bore this subtitle: *The Messiah Concept in the Old Testament and Later Judaism*. Note the abstract nouns "idea" and "concept" and the monolithic designations "Israel" and "Judaism." A recent collection of essays on the same topic that reflects the recognition of diversity within Second Temple Judaism is entitled *Judaisms and Their Messiahs at the Turn of the Christian Era.*[2] Note the plural nouns "Judaisms" and "Messiahs" and the absence of the abstract "idea" and "concept." The authors examine how the presence or absence of statements about the Messiah fits within the distinctive kind of Judaism being studied. Christian messianism is treated as one subdivision of late Second Temple Judaism.

The diversity within Second Temple Judaism allowed the emergence of what we today call Christianity. Jesus and his early followers did not set out to found a new religion. They continued to regard themselves as Jews by birth and life-style. Other Jews may have judged them to be peculiar or even dangerous. But they remained Jews. When Saul the Pharisee became Paul the Christian,[3] he shifted allegiance from one Judaism to another. But when Christian Judaism opened itself to non-Jews, it began to strain the limits of Jewish diversity. Some Christian Jews assumed that these Gentile Christians would also become Jews. Other Christian Jews, such as Paul, resisted imposing circumcision and the Torah upon Gentile Christians. Still other Jews regarded Jews like Paul as having apostasized from Judaism because of his life-style in consorting with Gentiles and his ideas about Jesus and those who may follow his way. Disagreement about the boundaries of Judaism and the limits of Jewish diversity provides the framework for Paul's own statements about Judaism.

The word "Judaism" derives from the geographical area Judah (or Judea) in the land of Israel—basically, the geographical area surrounding Jerusalem. In time, the name "Judean" (or Jew) was extended to those in other parts of the land of Israel (Galilee), and even to people scattered around the Mediterranean world in the so-called Diaspora who retained cultural, national, and religious ties to Judah.

Judaism in Paul's time was an international phenomenon. There were substantial Jewish populations in Rome, Damascus,

[2]Klausner (New York: Macmillan, 1955); Mowinckel (Nashville: Abingdon, 1956); *Judaisms and their Messiahs,* eds. J. Neusner, W. S. Green, and E. S. Frerichs (Cambridge-New York: Cambridge University Press, 1987).

[3]M. Hengel, *The Pre-Christian Paul* (London: SCM, 1990; Philadelphia: Trinity Press International).

Ephesus, Alexandria, and other great cities of the Roman Empire. These Jews had dealings with the local Gentiles and retained their connections with Judaism. Since they no longer lived in the land of Israel and could visit the Jerusalem Temple at most only occasionally, the Diaspora Jews gave special attention to the Scriptures. They produced and used as their Bible the Greek version known as the Septuagint. They developed religious, educational, cultural, and social centers known as synagogues. They (and their pagan neighbors) gave particular attention to the practices mandated in the Torah that made Jews different and gave them a distinct identity: circumcision, food laws and rules pertaining to ritual observance, and Sabbath regulations.

Paul was a Diaspora Jew. If we can trust the biographical data in Acts, Paul was born in Tarsus of Cilicia (Acts 9:11; 21:39; 22:3), on the southeastern coast of Asia Minor. Though living in a non-Jewish city, Paul grew up in a Jewish family and was initiated into Judaism through the Greek Bible. Two texts in Acts (22:3; 26:4-5) claim that Paul was also educated in Jerusalem under the Pharisee Gamaliel. There he became proficient in Pharisaism (see Phil 3:5), though he may well have come from an already Pharisaic family (see Acts 23:6).

Paul thus moved between the Diaspora and Jerusalem. But these were not entirely different worlds. All of Second Temple Judaism—including Jerusalem—was part of the larger Mediterranean culture.[4] The inroads of Hellenism were felt in Palestine from the late fourth century B.C. in economic matters, military strategy, language, and culture. Even the famous resistance to Hellenism undertaken in the second century B.C. by Judas Maccabeus and his brothers led ultimately to greater Hellenization, though the Maccabees did succeed in developing a distinctive form of Judaism. First-century Palestinian Judaism was not hermetically sealed off from its broader Greco-Roman environment.

Paul also describes himself as having been "a persecutor of the church" (Phil 3:6). What led the pre-Christian Paul to persecute Christians?[5] As a Greek-speaking Jew from the Diaspora, Paul

[4]Hengel, *Judaism and Hellenism. Studies in Their Encounter in Palestine during the Early Hellenistic Period* (Philadelphia: Fortress, 1974).

[5]Hengel, *The Pre-Christian Paul.*

probably had some association with the Greek-speaking "Hellenist" synagogues of Jerusalem. Such a synagogue may well have been Paul's spiritual and cultural home, however long he stayed in Jerusalem.

It seems that certain Hellenist Jews became Christians. If Acts 6–7 reflects any historical situation, it seems also that these Hellenistic-Jewish Christians were testing the limits of Judaism with radical views about the Jerusalem Temple and the Law. Such Christian Jews were the target of persecution in the land of Israel (Acts 8:1), whereas "the apostles" and, presumably, their followers were excepted (since as more conservative Christian Jews, they posed no threat). Among the Christian Hellenist Jews, the mission to the Gentiles in the Diaspora began (see Acts 11:19-21). The pre-Christian Paul was most likely dispatched by a Greek-speaking synagogue in Jerusalem to investigate what Christian Hellenist Jews were doing in Damascus and then to do something about stopping them. On his way to Damascus, according to Acts 9, 22, and 26, Paul had such a powerful experience of Jesus that he was transformed from a persecutor of the Church to an apostle of Christ Jesus. The impact of this experience on Paul's theology will be discussed in the next section.

What we know of Paul's public ministry was carried out in the cities of the Greco-Roman world. Pauline Christianity was an urban movement.[6] Paul, the Jew from Tarsus, exercised his Christian ministry as an apostle across the eastern and northern Mediterranean coasts, inland into Asia Minor and Greece, and as far as Rome (and with an eye toward Spain). In Acts, Paul's missionary activity in a city always begins with the Jewish community and the local synagogue and then moves out to the Gentiles. Even if this schema says more about Luke's theology than about Paul's practice, it does rest upon the likely assumption that Paul the Jew continued to make use of the communication network that existed among Diaspora Jews in the early stages of his apostolic work among Gentiles in a particular city.

Once having founded a Christian community and having moved on, Paul kept in touch with his converts by letters. These letters

---

[6]W. Meeks, *The First Urban Christians. The Social World of the Apostle Paul* (New Haven-London: Yale University Press, 1983).

are important indicators of Paul's Judaism. At the center, of course, is the death and resurrection of Jesus, and their implications for Jews and Gentiles. In arguing or developing a point, Paul quotes the Jewish Scriptures in their Greek version and applies the Jewish techniques of interpretation to them. But he also follows the conventions of Greco-Roman rhetoric in the broad outline of his letters. His letters generally contain an address or salutation, thanksgiving, body, and closing. Some such as Galatians have been analyzed according to the classical patterns of ancient rhetoric: epistolary prescript (1:1-5), introduction (1:6-11), statement of facts (1:12–2:14), proposition (2:15-21), proofs (3:1–4:31), exhortation (5:1–6:10), and epistolary postscript (6:11-18).[7]

The world of Paul the Diaspora Jew, who became a Christian, had many facets. His basic language was Greek. His Bible was the Septuagint. He knew and used Greco-Roman literary conventions. He worked in the cities of the Greco-Roman world. He spread the Christian gospel in the framework of a Judaism that was both diverse and international.

Paul's Theology

While Paul was very much a Diaspora Jew, it is futile to try to explain everything in his letters in terms of his background as a Jew in the Greco-Roman world. At one point in his life, Paul had a powerful experience of the risen Jesus that changed him radically. Whether that experience took precisely the dramatic forms in which it is described in Acts is neither affirmed nor denied by Paul himself. Paul was more interested in drawing out the implications of that experience than in telling how it happened.

One could appeal to many texts in Paul's letters for a summary of Pauline theology. Philippians 3:8-11 comes just after Paul's boasting over his Jewish heritage, his identity as a Pharisee, his work as a persecutor of the Church, and his careful and, indeed, blameless observance of the Law (3:5-6). All that he now regards as "loss" because of Christ (3:7). The transformative power of

[7]H. D. Betz, *Galatians. A Commentary on Paul's Letter to the Churches in Galatia* (Philadelphia: Fortress, 1979).

his experience of Christ's death and resurrection turned his life upside down:

> 8. More than that, I regard everything as loss because of the surpassing value of knowing Christ Jesus my Lord. For his sake I have suffered the loss of all things, and I regard them as rubbish, in order that I may gain Christ 9. and be found in him, not having a righteousness of my own that comes from the Law, but one that comes through faith in Christ, the righteousness from God based on faith. 10. I want to know Christ and the power of his resurrection and the sharing of his sufferings by becoming like him in his death, 11. if somehow I may attain the resurrection from the dead.

Paul's theology flows from the reversal of goals and values that came about from his encounter with the crucified and resurrected Christ. More accurate than the term "transformation" is the word "conformation" concealed in the translation of *symmorphizomenos* ("being formed with") in 3:10 as "becoming like." Paul understood Christ to be taking him over and reshaping him into the image of Christ. He regarded the identification between Christ and himself to be so complete that he could claim: "It is no longer I who live, but it is Christ who lives in me" (Gal 2:20).

As the result of being "conformed" to Christ, Paul the proud Jew and zealous Pharisee became the Apostle of Christ to the Gentiles. The one who had been blameless with respect to the Law now pursued the righteousness that comes through faith in Christ. The persecutor of the Church found meaning now only in the death and resurrection of Christ.

The seven undisputed letters that we have from Paul are the writings of a pastoral theologian. The theology included in them is usually in the service of resolving pastoral problems such as what to do with a runaway slave (Philemon), whether Christians may eat food offered to idols (1 Corinthians), how should Christians look upon the Roman Empire (Rom 13:1-7), and so forth. The letter to the Romans comes closest to a systematic treatise, but even it responds more or less directly (depending on one's interpretation) to tensions between Gentile and Jewish Christians at Rome.

The occasional and pastoral character of Paul's letters means that it is difficult to speak about his "theology" as if he were a professor of theology. There are some constants in Paul's theological outlook: the framework of Jewish apocalypticism, the saving and reconciling significance of Jesus' death and resurrection, the possibility for all people to participate in Christ, and the expectation that a certain kind of behavior is appropriate to one's status as a "new creation" in Christ. These elements are interconnected, and so it is difficult to single out one and hold it up as the "center" of Paul's theology. Furthermore, Paul the pastor was more concerned to point out the significance of these elements for the lives of his fellow Christians than he was to develop any one element in its proper philosophical and theological depth.

The letters that we have from Paul represent a relatively short span of time. The earliest (1 Thessalonians) comes from the early fifties of the first century A.D., and the latest (Romans, in my opinion) comes from the late fifties. A question that arises in nearly every study of a topic in Pauline theology is whether Paul's thought developed. Ten years or less is not a long span in which to chart a person's intellectual development, especially when the sources are "occasional" documents. Some interpreters argue that Paul's theology was embedded in his initial experience of Christ and so was all there from the beginning. Other interpreters maintain that on certain topics, it is possible to discern a development and a growth. One such topic is Paul's attitude toward Judaism. Paul certainly says very different things about Jews in 1 Thessalonians ("they displease God and oppose everyone," 2:15) and Romans ("all Israel will be saved" 11:26). But is the difference due to the development of Paul's thinking or the different situations that he addressed? The issue of Paul's theological development is as complicated as the quest for the center of his theology is.

Recognition of Paul as a pastoral theologian, giving advice to fellow Christians, makes a difference in the way we today read Paul. Augustine and Martin Luther surely rank among the great interpreters of Paul. And they have also taught us how to read Paul as the theologian of God's grace offered to sinful individuals. Thus, many serious readers of Paul's letters to the Galatians and Romans assume that Paul's central question is individualistic: How can I, as a sinful person, find mercy from a gracious God? There is a level at which Augustine and Luther were correct in interpreting Paul. But Paul himself was more interested in group and community problems.[8] Paul's question was more social ("How can Gentiles be part of the people of God?") than personal ("How can I as a sinner find forgiveness from an angry God?"). His individualistic and introspective comments were generally in the service of communal concerns, especially relations between Jewish Christians, other Jews, and Gentile Christians.

Paul the pastoral theologian was also a pioneer in Christian theology. His letters are full of fixed formulas, hymnic fragments, summaries of faith, and other traditions that give evidence of great theological vitality in the first two decades of Christian history (A.D. 30–50). Nevertheless, on many issues (e.g., the relevance of the Jewish Law), Paul gives the impression of boldly going to where no one had gone before. And sometimes the results are what we might expect from a theological pioneer: tensions and apparent inconsistencies, if not outright contradictions. On most issues, Paul is the "first word" rather than the "last word" in the New Testament.

[8]K. Stendahl, *Paul Among Jews and Gentiles* (Philadelphia: Fortress, 1976).

2

Before Romans

What are we to make of Paul's statements regarding his life as a Jew and Judaism in his letters other than Romans? On the one hand, Paul boasts about his life as a Jew: "I advanced in Judaism beyond many among my people of the same age, for I was far more zealous for the traditions of my ancestors" (Gal 1:14). . . . "Are they Hebrews? So am I. Are they Israelites? So am I. Are they descendants of Abraham? So am I" (2 Cor 11:22). . . . "circumcised on the eighth day, a member of the people of Israel, of the tribe of Benjamin, a Hebrew born of Hebrews; as to the Law, a Pharisee; as to zeal, a persecutor of the church; as to righteousness under the Law, blameless" (Phil 3:5-6). On the other hand, Paul vigorously denies that right relationship with God comes about through observance of the Law and declares all his credentials and achievements as a Jew to be "loss" and even "rubbish" (Phil 3:7-8). What are we to make of such statements?

To make any sense of them, we must read them in their contexts in the letters in which they appear. In the four letters examined here, Paul addresses Christian communities that he himself had founded: those of the Thessalonians, the Galatians, the Corinthians, and the Philippians. The Christians to whom he wrote were mainly, if not entirely, Gentile Christians; that is, they were not Jews. Paul had brought these people to Christianity without obliging them to be circumcised or to observe Jewish laws such as food rules and Sabbath rest. Some of Paul's fellow Jewish Christians were convinced that the practice of Paul and other missionaries to the Gentiles was mistaken. They contended that Gentiles had to become Jews to be real Christians. In other words, they looked upon Christianity as a sect within Judaism.

Paul had another idea. He did not regard Christianity as an independent religion separate from Israel. But he defined Israel so as to include not only Jewish Christians like himself but also Gentile Christians, and traced this "Israel of God" (Gal 6:16) back to Abraham.

Gentile Christianity was not Paul's invention (see Acts 10–11). Moreover, the Jerusalem apostles agreed that Gentiles could forgo circumcision (see Gal 2:1-10) and needed only to observe a few basic precepts of the Law (see Acts 15:20, 29).

That political compromise, however, raised still another question: Were there to be two kinds of Christianity—one for Jews, the other for Gentiles? Paul's Jewish Christian opponents contended that there was only one kind—Jewish Christianity. When they tried to convince Paul's Gentile Christians about this, Paul reacted vigorously to protect what he considered the gospel of freedom that he himself experienced and preached.

These debates involving Paul the Jew, the Gentile Christians addressed in the letters, and the Jewish Christians in the background are the context of much of what Paul said about his life as a Jew and about Judaism. Yet before we get into these debates, we first need to look at some apparently nasty things that Paul said about other Jews (not Jewish Christians) in 1 Thessalonians.

1 Thessalonians 2:14-16

The Church at Thessalonica, a port city in northeastern Greece, had been founded by Paul (see Acts 17:1-9). Paul wrote 1 Thessalonians (generally acknowledged to be the oldest complete document in the New Testament) in A.D. 51–52 to respond to some problems reported to him by Timothy (see 1 Thess 2:17–3:10). He gave particular attention to the Thessalonians' misunderstandings regarding the fate of the dead (see 4:13–5:11).

The Thessalonian Christians were largely, if not entirely, Gentile. Paul celebrates the fact that they "turned to God from idols"

(1:9). He uses no direct quotations from the Old Testament, though there may be some allusions. According to Acts 17:1-9, the Jews at Thessalonica were jealous of Paul's success as a Christian missionary among both Jews and Gentiles: "Some of them were persuaded and joined Paul and Silas, as did a great many of the devout Greeks and not a few of the leading women" (Acts 17:4). In reaction, "the Jews" stirred up a mob against the Christian missionaries and their converts. This tension between Jews and Christians at Thessalonica provides the background for one of the most apparently negative passages about Jews in the New Testament (1 Thess 2:14-16).

1 Thessalonians is unusual among Paul's letters because it contains two long passages of thanksgiving (1:2-2:12; 2:13-3:13)—more than half the letter. The pertinent text comes at the beginning of the second thanksgiving:

> 14. For you, brothers and sisters, became imitators of the churches of God in Christ Jesus that are in Judea, for you suffered the same things from your own compatriots as they did from the Jews, 15. who killed both the Lord Jesus and the prophets, and drove us out; they displease God and oppose everyone 16. by hindering us from speaking to the Gentiles so that they may be saved. Thus they have constantly been filling up the measure of their sins; but God's wrath has overtaken them at last.

According to Paul, the Thessalonian Christians were now imitating the experience of the Christians in Judea (Jerusalem and environs) in suffering for the gospel. Paul goes on in 2:15 to accuse "the Jews" of having killed Jesus and the prophets, of driving Paul out, and of opposing God and human beings by preventing the Christian mission. He imagines a kind of quota of sins to be filled before God acts (see 2 Macc 6:14-15) and adds that "God's wrath" has already overtaken them.

On the surface, this text is a devastating indictment of "the Jews." It presents them as "Christ-killers" and suggests that their sufferings are just recompense from God for their evil deeds. This is indeed a "dangerous" text in Christian-Jewish relations.

It is necessary, however, to go beneath the surface. The "Jews" are *Ioudaioi*, the inhabitants of Judea. Paul in 1 Thessalonians

2:14-16 is clearly talking about Judeans in a geographical sense, since what he describes took place around Jerusalem. Paul, an ethnic Jew (though not a Judean), is talking about those Judeans who opposed Jesus and the Jewish Christians in Judea. Moreover, Paul's harsh language is typical of the polemics used by philosophers and religious people in the Greco-Roman world.[1] The charge that Jews "oppose everyone" was commonplace. Also, Paul draws upon the Old Testament tradition of prophetic denunciation here.

Who is being denounced? Between verses 14 and 15, the NRSV (and most other translations) places a comma. The original Greek text, of course, had no punctuation (or even spaces between letters). On the presence of this comma much hangs, since it suggests that all Judeans or Jews did what is listed in 2:15-16a. Without the comma, the sentence restricts the misdeeds to those Jews who killed Jesus and the prophets, and drove Paul out. It is fair to speak about the "anti-Semitic comma" between verses 14 and 15.[2]

Furthermore, there are strong arguments (though no textual evidence) that 2:14-16 was a later addition, not part of the original text.[3] If the reader moves directly from 2:13 to 2:17, the transition is smooth and coherent. The fact is that 2:14-16 interrupts the flow of Paul's argument and gives the impression of being an interruption. Moreover, the catastrophe alluded to in 2:16b ("God's wrath has overtaken them at last") sounds like a description of the destruction of Jerusalem in A.D. 70—some twenty years after the composition of 1 Thessalonians. It could conceivably refer to the famine described in Acts 11:27-30 or some local calamity in Jerusalem before A.D. 50. But it still sounds most like what happened in A.D. 70.

Careful analysis of 1 Thessalonians 2:14-16 leads one to play down its significance for understanding Paul's attitude toward Jews and Judaism. It may be a later interpolation, not written

[1]L. T. Johnson, "The New Testament's Anti-Jewish Slander and the Conventions of Ancient Polemic," *Journal of Biblical Literature* 108 (1989) 419–41.

[2]F. D. Gilliard, "The Problem of the Antisemitic Comma between 1 Thessalonians 2:14 and 15," *New Testament Studies* 35 (1989) 481–502.

[3]B. A. Pearson, "1 Thessalonians 2:13-16: A Deutero-Pauline Interpolation," *Harvard Theological Review* 64 (1971) 79–94.

by Paul at all but by some scribe. Even if it was part of Paul's own text, not too much should be made out of it. When taken out of context, it sounds very anti-Jewish. But when read in its proper historical setting, it has the Jew Paul comparing the opposition suffered by Gentile Christians at Thessalonica to the persecution suffered by Christian Jews in Judea. Paul holds certain Jews (omitting the "anti-Semitic comma") responsible for Jesus' death and the persecution of Christians in Judea. He regards some local catastrophe as punishment for the sins of those certain Judeans in opposing the gospel.

There are too many problems associated with 1 Thessalonians 2:14-16. If we wish to grasp Paul's understanding of Jews and Judaism, we need to look at other texts.

Galatians 1–2

The issue of Paul's attitude toward Jews and Judaism is more central in his letter to the Galatians (around A.D. 54). Yet even here, we get only an oblique perspective, since Paul's opponents appear to be Jewish Christians and not other Jews. Paul had brought the gospel to the Galatians, the descendants of Celts who settled in Asia Minor. In keeping with his gospel, Paul did not impose on these Gentile Christians the obligation to become Jews, that is, to be circumcised and to observe the Law. But certain Jewish Christians contended that Paul's gospel was incorrect and that Gentile Christians had to "go through" Judaism in order to become full-fledged Christians. What were the Gentile Christians at Galatia to do? To whom should they listen? Which gospel were they to follow?

Paul wrote to the Galatians as their founder and their pastor (though now at a distance). He wrote to vindicate both his gospel and his apostleship. It is imperative to bear in mind that his opponents were not Jews in general, but Christian Jews who sought to make conversion to Judaism an entrance requirement to the Church for Gentile Christians.

This quite specific purpose explains why, in the salutation (Gal 1:1-5), Paul insisted on the divine origin of his apostleship ("neither by human commission nor from human authorities," 1:1) and summarized his teaching about Jesus ("who gave himself for our sins to set us free from the present evil age," 1:4). It also explains why, instead of the customary thanksgiving section (as in 1 Thess 1:2-3:13), Paul went straight to the matter: The Galatian Christians "are turning to a different gospel" (1:6), which Paul regarded as confusion and perversion of the gospel that he had preached.

The stories that Paul tells in the narrative segment of his letter (1:12-2:21) are presented not merely as interesting or ingratiating personal experiences, but rather seek to bolster Paul's claim that "the gospel that was proclaimed by me is not of human origin" (1:11). There was nothing in Paul's gospel that made it necessary for Gentile Christians to be circumcised or to observe the Torah.

The first section (1:12-24) insists that Paul's circumcision-free and Law-free gospel for Gentiles originated in "a revelation of Jesus Christ" (1:12). It cannot be traced to his "life in Judaism" for then he was an eager persecutor of Christianity (1:13-14). Nor did Paul get his gospel from the other apostles since he had no contact with them until three years after his turn to Christianity (1:17-24). Rather, his commission to proclaim Christ among the Gentiles (1:15-16) came directly from God.

The second section (2:1-10) indicates that Paul's proclamation of the gospel to the Gentiles was approved by the Jerusalem leaders. Fourteen years later (after the first revelation [A.D. 36] or after the first visit to Jerusalem [A.D. 39]?), Paul went up to Jerusalem again and laid out before the leaders there the gospel that he had been preaching (2:2). Since they did not force the Gentile Titus to be circumcised, the Jerusalem leaders presumably agreed with Paul that Gentile Christians had no obligation to become fully Jewish. Though there was opposition from Jewish Christian rigorists, Paul resisted for the sake of the "truth of the gospel" (2:4-5).

The major issue at the Jerusalem conference, as it is described by Paul, was circumcision. The result of the conference seems to have been a division of missionary labor. Paul and Barnabas would bring the gospel to the uncircumcised (Gentiles), and Peter and others would bring the gospel to the circumcised (Jews). The only condition laid upon Paul's mission was that he be mindful of the "poor" (most likely, the Christians in Jerusalem) as he went about his mission (2:10). Paul, at least, understood this division of labor as approval for his circumcision-free gospel for Gentiles. Thus, he offers it as proof to the Galatians that they were being misinformed by Paul's Jewish-Christian opponents who wanted them to adopt circumcision.

The decision of the Jerusalem conference seemed like a reasonable compromise and a politically effective solution to a serious problem within early Christianity. But as is the case with most political compromises, the agreement contained the seed of still another conflict. The Jerusalem conference in effect seemed to create two kinds of Christianity: Jewish Christianity, and Gentile Christianity. How then were these two kinds of Christians to interact? What relationship should exist between them? The matter came to a head in the incident at Antioch described in Galatians 2:11-14.

Whereas the issue at Jerusalem had been circumcision, the issue at Antioch was Jews and Gentiles sharing a common table. Cephas (presumably the same as Peter) freely ate with Gentiles at Antioch until some stricter Jewish Christians came from James in Jerusalem. Then Cephas and other Jewish Christians (even Barnabas!) backed off out of respect for the "kosher" laws of Leviticus 17:10-16. The implication of their action suggests that the "Jerusalem compromise" in effect demanded two kinds of Christianities and a segregation between Jews and Gentiles even though both were Christians.

Strict logic would seem to have been on the side of Cephas, James, and the other Jewish Christians. At least, segregated Christianities would appear to follow from the decision reached about circumcision in Jerusalem. Paul did not see it that way! Instead, Paul characterizes the withdrawal of his fellow Jewish Christians as "hypocrisy" (2:13). He also suggests that Cephas had already begun to "live like a Gentile and not like a Jew" (2:14)—referring perhaps merely to his sharing a common table at Antioch or possibly to his more thoroughgoing abandonment of Jewish customs.

In 2:15-21, Paul makes the issue into one of theology in which the gospel itself is at stake. The question as Paul sees it is this: What brings about right relationship with God (justification)? Is it the "works of the Law" (circumcision, food laws, Sabbath observance, and so forth)⁴ or the faith of (or in) Christ?⁵ For Paul, of course, it is the latter. It is not clear that any Jew would have embraced the former option, since in Jewish theology, observing the Law is a response to God's gracious love offered in covenantal relationship with Israel. Paul, however, seems to have perceived a radical disjunction between the works of the Law and faith in (or, of) Christ. At least, he claims to have torn down the works of the Law (2:18) and to have died to the Law (2:19), thus suggesting that he no longer observed parts of the Law.

Paul regarded Christ as now the way to God and to God's righteousness (2:19-21). On the theoretical level, Paul considered the "works of the Law" as a rival to Christ, and, therefore, he felt compelled to argue for the superiority of Christ over them. On the practical level, Paul viewed the works of the Law as matters of indifference. When ministering to Jews, Paul became "as one under the Law" (1 Cor 9:20), and when ministering to Gentiles, he became "as one outside the Law" (1 Cor 9:21). Since much of his later ministry was devoted to Gentiles, it is fair to assume that Paul shared the life of Gentile Christians and felt no obligation to observe certain elements of the Jewish Law. His freedom in this regard was based on what he maintained was the overwhelming value of the gospel.

The narrative segment of Galatians (1:12-2:21) concerns a series of conflicts within Christianity that have implications for the ways that Christians came to look upon Jews and Judaism. Where did Paul get his circumcision-free and Law-free gospel for Gentiles? By divine revelation is Paul's claim in 1:12-24. Do Gentile Christians need to be circumcised? The answer is no from both Paul and the "pillar" apostles at Jerusalem, though there were some conservative dissenters on this matter (2:1-10). May Jewish Christians and Gentile Christians live in the same community? Though

---

⁴J. D. G. Dunn, "Works of the Law and the Curse of the Law (Galatians 3:10-14)," *New Testament Studies* 31 (1985) 523-42.

⁵See L. T. Johnson "Rom 3:21-26 and the Faith of Jesus," *Catholic Biblical Quarterly* 44 (1982) 77-90; S. K. Williams, "Again *Pistis Christou*," *CBQ* 49 (1987) 431-47; L. Ramaroson, "La justification par la foi *du* Christ Jesus," *Science et Esprit* 39 (1987) 81-92. All three articles defend the subjective genitive. I agree with their judgment. But in what is quoted from the NRSV I have observed its objective genitive translation. It would require another book to adjudicate this dispute.

Jewish Christians wavered and eventually said no, Paul made his yes into a matter of theological principle and accused his fellow Jewish Christians of hypocrisy on this issue (2:11-21).

Paul's position eventually won the argument. Or, perhaps better stated, when Gentiles came to dominate in the church, they looked to Paul's letters as the theological basis for their neglect of much of the Law and their insistence on one kind (Gentile) of Christianity. But in the mid-fifties of the first century, Paul's position on the Antioch controversy probably seemed illogical in light of the Jerusalem conference's decision to allow two kinds of Christianity. Nor is it at all clear that Paul's position was immediately or widely accepted.

Galatians 3-4

In the narrative section in chapters 1-2, Paul concluded that justification comes not by the works of the Law, but through faith in Jesus Christ (2:16). In chapters 3-4, Paul seeks to prove his case by appealing to the experience of the Gentile Christians in Galatia and to the Scriptures.

First the experience of the Gentile Christians. In reading Galatians, one must never lose sight of Paul's audience (Gentile Christians brought to faith by Paul) and his opponents (Jewish Christians who contended that Gentiles needed to take on Judaism as they became Christians). It appears that some Gentile Christians were being convinced that the Jewish Christians were correct and that Paul had "shortchanged" them. In this setting, Paul's question to the Gentile Christians at Galatia goes straight to the matter at hand: "Did you receive the Spirit by doing the works of the Law or by believing what you heard?" (3:2). Both they and Paul agree that the Galatian Christians have already received the Spirit. What is at issue is, How? Since Paul had not imposed the Jewish Law upon them, it could not have been "by doing the works of the Law." It must have been by "believing what you heard."

Paul also appeals to the ambiguity of the Greek word *pneuma* ("spirit"), which refers to both the Holy Spirit and the "spiritual" aspect of the person. In the contrast between "Spirit-spirit" and "flesh," Paul aligns the works of the Law with the flesh: "Having started with the Spirit, are you now ending with the flesh?" (3:3). So, according to Paul, the Galatian Christians came to receive the Spirit without the Law and so have no need of it now. In fact, for them to embrace the Law would be a step backward into the realm of the flesh.

The challenge facing Paul in the rest of Galatians 3-4 is to show how the Galatians' experience is consistent with the Old Testament Scriptures. To do so, Paul emphasizes faith (with Abraham as a model) as the principle constituting the people of God and argues that, at least for Gentile Christians, the Law was of historical value only and has no present or existential significance. These are unusual arguments from a Jew in any age. They bear witness to the overwhelming character of Paul's experience of Christ, which in turn made everything else of inferior status and secondary importance.

The complicated argument in Galatians 3:6-29 shows that the true children of Abraham are people of faith. In 3:6-9, Paul appeals to Genesis 15:6 to show that faith is the principle of righteousness before God, and to Genesis 12:3 and 18:18 to show that Gentiles are included among Abraham's children and can share in what was promised to him. Then in 3:10-14, Paul appeals to various Old Testament texts (Deut 27:26; Hab 2:4; Lev 18:5; Deut 21:23) to confirm that right relationship with God comes not through the works of the Law, but through faith. Next in 3:15-18, Paul appeals to God's promise to Abraham in Genesis 13:15 (see 17:8; 24:7) to show that Abraham's "seed" and heir is Christ, and that the gift of the Law on Sinai did not annul or add to the promise made to Abraham.

Why then the Law? What purpose did it have? Paul deals with this question in 3:19-26. He clearly regards the Law as inferior to the promise made to Abraham and as serving at best some auxiliary purposes. The Law helped people to recognize what sin is, served as a provisional guide until Christ came, and helped put all people under the reign of sin (3:19-20, 22). Though surely not contrary to the promise, the Law ought not to be confused with the promise, nor should one assume that it can bring about right relationship with God. The Law functioned as a "pedagogue" ("disciplinarian") who accompanied the child to school and oversaw the child's education (3:24-25). But with the coming of Christ, the pedagogical function of the Law is no longer necessary. Now all can be "children of God through faith" (3:26). Paul concludes that all—Jew and Greek, slave and free, male and female—belong to Christ and therefore are Abraham's children.

The temporary, historical value of the Law is brought out by an analogy in 4:1-3: Just as orphaned children are under the guardianship of trustees until the time appointed by their father, so we have been under the "elemental spirits"—among which Paul places the Law (see 4:3, 9). But now that Christ's coming has marked the time appointed for the end of the guardianship, it is the time for enjoying the legal inheritance (4:4-7). The Son redeemed "those who were under the Law" (4:5)—not merely Jews but all people who found themselves under the power of sin and death, aided and abetted by the Law. This is a very negative approach to the Law, according to which it had only temporary value and was an integral part of the "problem" that Christ came to resolve.

In 4:8-20, Paul applies these reflections to the Gentile Christians at Galatia. For them to fall prey to the attractions of Jewish Christianity would mean a fall back into spiritual slavery (4:9) and make Paul's apostolic activity into a waste (4:11). Here Paul places the Galatians' former paganism on the same level as Law-observing Judaism (and apparently, also, Jewish Christianity).

In 4:12, Paul begs the Galatians to "become as I am, for I also have become as you are." This statement seems to suggest that Paul has put aside observance of the Torah and to warn Gentile Christians not to be enticed into Torah observance. Paul goes on to recall his first encounter with the Galatians and their enthusiastic reception of his gospel (4:13-16). He then criticizes his Jewish Christian rivals by casting doubt on their real motives (4:17-20).

Paul's fondness for dialectical thinking, already shown in Galatians 3:1-5 (Law versus faith, flesh versus spirit), appears in the allegory of Sarah and Hagar in 4:21-31. On the one side, there is slavery embodied in Hagar the slave, her children, the flesh, the Sinai covenant, and the present Jerusalem. On the other side, there is freedom embodied in Sarah, her children, the promise, the Abrahamic covenant, and the Jerusalem above. Paul identifies himself with the Gentile Christians ("we") as children of the promise, and suggests that those who continue to observe the Sinai covenant are children of the slave (4:31).

In Galatians 3-4, the focus has shifted. Whereas in chapter 2, Paul was concerned about the specific issues of circumcision of Gentile Christians (2:1-10) and a common table for Jewish and Gentile Christians (2:11-14), in chapters 3-4 he directly confronts the general issue of the Sinai Law itself. Though quite negative in his assessment he can see the glimmer of a positive value in its provisional function of "disciplinarian" (3:24-25). But on the whole, the Law is part of the problem, not part of the solution. It is allied with the flesh (3:3), sin (3:19-22), the elemental spirits (4:3, 9), and servitude (4:21-31). Paul himself seems no longer to observe it (4:12) and warns Gentile Christians against taking up its practice.

The target of Paul's remarks in Galatians is a kind of Jewish Christianity that would impose the obligations of Judaism on Gentile Christians. This movement threatened to tear down Paul's missionary work among the Galatians and called into question his gospel. The concrete, polemical situation must not be forgotten. Paul is not arguing about Judaism but about the feasibility of Jewish Christianity for Gentiles. Nevertheless, what Paul says in Galatians manifests a radical devaluation of the Torah and something of a redefinition of the people of God (people of faith after the pattern of Abraham). What Paul says leaves little opening for other Jews who follow the Torah and do not profess faith in Christ.

2 Corinthians 3

There is a sharp break in content and tone between chapters 1-9 and 10-13 in 2 Corinthians. Many interpreters regard the letter as a combination of two (or even more) shorter letters. But in both major parts, Paul felt the need to defend his apostleship. As in Galatians, the attacks on Paul seem to have come from Jewish Christians who objected to his Law-free gospel for Gentiles. Against such opponents, Paul identifies himself as a Hebrew, an

Israelite, and a descendant of Abraham (2 Cor 11:22). Whether there were Jewish-Christian missionaries actually in Corinth is not clear. At any rate, at least their complaints against Paul and his gospel had made their way to Corinth.

As in Galatians 3–4, Paul appeals first to the experience of the Gentile Christians at Corinth and then to the Scriptures. Paul begins in 3:1-3 by alluding to the practice of showing letters of introduction and recommendation upon arriving at a new place (see the case of Phoebe in Rom 16:1-2). Perhaps Paul's opponents had produced a letter of recommendation from the Jerusalem Church. But Paul has a better letter of recommendation: the Corinthian Christians themselves ("you yourselves are our letter"). They form a living letter "written on our hearts, to be known and read by all . . . a letter of Christ, prepared by us, written . . . with the Spirit of the living God, not on tablets of stone but on tablets of human hearts" (3:2-3).

The way in which the living letter of recommendation is described alludes to the promise in Jeremiah 31:33: "I will put my law within them, and I will write it on their hearts." Just as Israelites returned from exile would fully internalize the Torah so that they would no longer need teachers or external texts, so the Gentile Christians at Corinth had fully internalized the gospel.

The same text from Jeremiah also contains the promise of a "new covenant" (Jer 31:31), which introduces the scriptural part in Paul's argument. The "new covenant" is not as prominent a New Testament theme as most people suppose.[6] Apart from 2 Corinthians 3, it appears in Hebrews 8:7-13 and the "words of institution" at the Last Supper (Matt 26:28 parr.). The Essenes, who gave us the Dead Sea scrolls, used it to describe their own place within Jewish life (see especially *Damascus Document*). It may have been part of the theological vocabulary used by Paul's Jewish Christian opponents. At any rate, Paul does not do much with the idea elsewhere. And what he does with it in 2 Corinthians 3 is not easy to understand.

The Scripture texts are Jeremiah 31:31-34 (by way of allusion) and Exodus 34:29-35 (more extensive treatment). Paul's method is dialectic—finding contrasts, indeed polar opposites.

---

[6]G. Lohfink, *The Covenant Never Revoked* (New York: Paulist, 1991).

Paul claims to be a minister of "the new covenant" (3:6) . With the words of Jeremiah 31:31-34 in the background, he draws the following contrasts: tablets of stone versus tablets of human hearts (3:3); old covenant (3:14) versus new covenant (3:6); letter versus spirit (3:6); and "the letter kills" versus "the Spirit gives life" (3:6).

The contrasts are clearly drawn. But what is being contrasted? To what do these contrasts refer?

The same dialectical method is then applied to Exodus 34:29-35, which describes how Moses' face shone so brightly because of his encounter with God on Sinai that he had to put on a veil after speaking to the people of Israel lest he frighten them with his dazzling brilliance. The contrast that Paul draws out in 2 Corinthians 3:7-11 is between the ministry of death/condemnation (3:7, 9) and the ministry of the Spirit/justification (3:8, 9). It is clearly between the (Sinai) Law (which, in Paul's interpretation, was the ally of death and condemnation) and the gospel (which brought the Spirit and right relationship with God).

Paul does not deny that glory surrounded the Sinai covenant. But the glory surrounding Christ and the gospel is even more brilliant (3:8, 9) and is permanent (3:11) as opposed to transitory. As in Galatians 3–4, Paul plays down the importance of the Sinai covenant with respect to the more basic relationship between God and God's people that began with Abraham. He separates the Law from the promise and presents it as at best a pale anticipation of the greater glory to come with Christ.

What about the mysterious veil of Moses? Paul, in 2 Cor 3:12-18, finds in it more material for his dialectic of contrasts. First, in 3:12-13, the veil over Moses' face contrasts with the boldness that characterizes Paul's proclamation of the gospel. Then, in 3:14-18, the veil functions as a device to prevent the people of Israel from really understanding the true meaning of the "Old covenant." That term refers not so much to the "Old Testament" as a book as it does to the biblical accounts of the Sinai covenant ("when they hear the reading of the old covenant . . . whenever Moses is read").

Paul contends that, when non-Christian Jews (and perhaps even Law-observant Jewish Christians) read the Sinai material, they fail to understand it properly. They fail because "their minds were hardened" (3:14) and "a veil lies over their minds" (3:15). He also contends "when one turns to the Lord (= Christ), the veil is removed." As in Galatians 3, Christ is the key to the Hebrew Scriptures. When those Scriptures are read in the light of Christ, the veil is set aside (3:14). Paul suggests that the Sinai covenant consists of types or shadows pointing to Christ, and was at best of temporary historical value and at worst an ally of sin and death. Now, with the coming of Christ, it is possible to enjoy the Spirit, the glory of the Lord, and freedom (3:17-18).

As in Galatians 3-4, Paul in 2 Corinthians 3 appeals to the experience of Gentile Christians ("a letter of Christ") to explain why they do not need to observe the Law. Likewise, Paul interprets the Scriptures to mean that the old (= Sinai) covenant was inferior to the "new" covenant in Christ and only temporary in validity. Paul probably did not set out here to make a statement about "Judaism." Rather, he wanted to answer the charges of his Jewish Christian opponents that, by neglecting the Sinai Law, Paul was keeping Gentiles from "full" Christianity. Paul denied the principle set forth by his fellow Jewish Christians. In doing so, however, he introduced some very negative stereotypes about all Law-observing Jews: They belong to the "old" covenant, and their minds are hardened and veiled so that they do not even understand the Scriptures they prize so highly.

Philippians 3

Paul had brought Christianity to Philippi, a Roman colony in northern Greece (see Acts 16:12-40). His letter to the Philippians was probably written about the same time as 2 Corinthians (mid-fifties). It too may well be a collection of several letters, with chapter 3 constituting an originally separate piece. In chapter 3, there is no indication that Paul is a prisoner, and the tone changes from encouragement to attack. The attack from Paul presupposes pressure from Jewish-Christian missionaries who insisted that Gentile Christians undergo circumcision and observe the Law (as in Galatians and 2 Corinthians).

Philippians 3 helps to explain why Paul no longer regarded circumcision and Torah observance to be important. He had un-
dergone a "transformation," or more accurately, a "conformation" to Christ. The weak NRSV translation of *symmorphizomenos* ("becoming like him") in 3:10 scarcely does justice to the
powerful idea expressed there. Paul had taken on the "form"
(*morphē*) of Christ (see Phil 2:6). He had become "formed along
with" Christ in his death (through baptism) in the hope of sharing his resurrection. In 3:20-21, the goal of Christian life is presented as total "conformity" to Christ: "He will transform the
body of our humiliation that it may be conformed to the body
of his glory. . . ." This idea of "conformity" to Christ is at the
root of Paul's statement in Gal 2:20: "It is no longer I who live,
but it is Christ who lives in me."

There is a longstanding debate about whether it is proper to
call Paul a convert.[7] If conversion implies moving from one religion to another, Paul was not a convert, since in his own eyes
(and some others), he remained a Jew. But if conversion applies
to moving from one kind of Judaism (Pharisaism) to another
(Christianity), then Paul was a convert.

Paul the Pharisee had sought right relationship with God in
the sphere of the Torah. His credentials as a Jew were in perfect
order: "circumcised on the eighth day, a member of the people
of Israel, of the tribe of Benjamin, a Hebrew born of Hebrews;
as to the Law a Pharisee; as to zeal, a persecutor of the church;
as to righteousness under the Law, blameless" (3:5-6). Paul the
Christian, however, found right relationship with God in Christ's
death and resurrection (3:9-11). With this discovery, he came to
recognize that faith is the sphere in which both Jews and Gentiles find right relationship with God. This recognition—that being
"conformed" to Christ (and not the works of the Law) is the way
to God's righteousness—provided the theological basis for insist-
ing that Gentile Christians need not be forced to go through Judaism in order to become full Christians and members of God's
people.

Paul's positive recognition of what happened to him in being
"conformed" to Christ is the foundation for his attacks on his

---

[7]See the full discussion on pp. 70–71.

Jewish Christian opponents and his apparently disparaging remarks about Judaism in Philippians 3.

Paul begins his warning in a brutal way: "Beware of the dogs, beware of the evil workers, beware of those who mutilate the flesh" (3:2). Paul addresses Gentile Christians. The term "dogs" alludes to the Jewish (and Jewish-Christian) way of referring contemptuously to Gentiles (see Matt 15:26-27). Thus, Paul was probably throwing back at the Jewish Christians their own assessment of Gentiles. By calling them "the evil workers," Paul may also have been alluding to the Jewish-Christian insistence on the "works" of the Law; see 2 Corinthians 11:13 where they are called "deceitful workers." Their insistence on circumcision (*peritomē*) is countered by Paul's description of it as "mutilation" (*katatomē*). Paul then redefines circumcision by applying it to those who worship in the Spirit, boast in Christ, and do not put their trust in the flesh (3:3). Thus, he can say "we are the circumcision" and include Gentile Christians within his definition (see Rom 2:27-29; 4:11-12; Gal 6:12-13).

Paul goes on the attack again in 3:18-19: "For many live as enemies of the cross of Christ. . . . Their end is destruction; their god is the belly; and their glory is in their shame; their minds are set on earthly things." Though it is hard for us today to imagine Paul calling other Jewish Christians "enemies of the cross," the most straightforward reading of Philippians 3 assumes that the opponents were the same throughout. They were Jewish Christians who insisted that Gentiles be circumcised ("their glory is in their shame") and obey the Jewish dietary laws ("whose god is the belly"). Paul dismisses their program as concerned with "earthly things."

Paul's assessment of his birth into and former life in Judaism (Phil 3:5-6; see Gal 1:13) did not proceed from a guilty conscience. In fact, he proclaims himself "blameless" with respect to righteousness under the Law (3:6). But with his new relationship to God through Christ, Paul came to re-evaluate his life. What had been important (his birth as a Jew and his progress in Judaism), he now considered to be without value. The Church that he had persecuted he now embraced. The surpassing value of knowing Christ led Paul to reckon his former privileges and achievements to be "rubbish" (3:8).

Paul's language in Philippians 3 is often brutal when he attacks his Jewish-Christian opponents and reflects on his past in light of his present. Yet, the strength of Paul's language testifies to the power of his positive experience of Christ. That experience apparently convinced him that membership in God's people was available to all—Gentiles and Jews alike.

Conclusion

In the letters studied so far, Paul has made no direct pronouncement regarding non-Christian Jews or Judaism apart from Christ. Paul appears as a pastoral theologian, trying to illumine and resolve the problems facing Gentile Christians and caused by Jewish Christian critics of Paul's gospel.

Nothing that Paul says about his life as a Jew and Judaism makes sense apart from his transformative experience of Christ. He was convinced that he was being "conformed" to Christ's death and resurrection, and that now Christ lived within him. This positive experience led him to redefine membership in God's people to include all men and women of faith after the model of Abraham. It led him, also, to regard circumcision and other elements of the Law as unnecessary for Gentiles and of secondary importance for Jews.

Did Paul still regard himself as a Jew? He surely did. But he traced his Jewish heritage to Abraham, not to Moses on Sinai. Did Paul still observe the Jewish Law? As the apostle sent to Gentile Christians, Paul lived with Gentiles and may not have observed all the prescriptions of the Torah. In dealing with Jews, Paul may well have lived a full Jewish life (see 1 Cor 9:20). Yet, he did not regard Law-observance as incumbent upon him: "I myself am not under the law" (1 Cor 9:20). And in urging the Galatian Christians to resist observing the Jewish Law, Paul probably admits that he gave up Law-observance, at least in Gentile company: "Become as I am, for I also have become as you are" (Gal 4:12).

What was Paul's problem with the Law? The basic problem was that it did not and could not do for him what his experience of Christ had done for him—bring him into what he regarded as right relationship with God. Paul had tried both ways to God, and found the way of Torah lacking and Christ to be the fullness of his hopes. Therefore, he sought to warn Gentiles of the secondary importance of and even potential dangers in the way of Torah.

3

Romans

Practically everything in Romans is pertinent to Paul's attitudes toward Jews and Judaism. In a short book, one must be selective. So, I will focus on the texts that seem most pertinent to the major theme. These texts concern why Jews needed the revelation of God's righteousness in Christ (2:1–3:20) and the mystery of the Jewish rejection of the gospel (9–11). In between these two discussions, I will look briefly at what Paul says in chapters 4–8 about the consequences of Jesus' death and resurrection. Thus, I will treat the plight of Jews apart from Christ (2:1–3:20), Christ the solution (4–8), and the mystery of Israel (9–11). The conclusion to Paul's meditation on the mystery of Israel (11:25-32) is so significant for our issue, however, that it will be treated in a separate chapter following this one. But before turning to these texts, we need to place them in their historical setting and in their theological context in the argument of Romans.

The Occasion

Paul's letter to the Romans looks more like a synthesis of Paul's gospel than any of his other letters do. Nevertheless, the occasion for his writing to the Romans was very concrete: Paul wanted to make Rome the base of his mission in the West and from there move on to Spain (see Rom 15:24, 28). He was really asking for a place to stay and an opportunity to get to know the Christians at Rome (1:11-15), who had surely already heard of Paul. Thus, Paul may have intended his letter to the Romans as a formal but preliminary statement of his gospel to avert misunderstandings and to undercut rumors at Rome. He may also have wanted to organize the content of his preaching before beginning the western phase of his mission that would take him as far as Spain.

Yet, before Paul could go to Rome or to Spain, he first had to bring the proceeds of the great collection to the leaders of the Church at Jerusalem (see 2 Cor 8–9). It is entirely possible that, in addition to presenting the collection for the "poor," Paul foresaw that he would be expected to defend his Law-free gospel for Gentiles before the Jewish Christians of the Jerusalem community. Thus, Romans can be viewed as a "dress rehearsal" for what Paul expected to say at Jerusalem.

This way of reading Romans—as a theological synthesis—views the letter as composed in anticipation of a personal visit (to Rome), of further missionary activity (in Spain), or of an interrogation by Church officials (at Jerusalem). It is also possible, and perhaps even preferable, to read Romans as addressing more directly the internal problems among the Roman Christians. And those internal problems appear to have been rooted in the tensions between Gentile Christians and Jewish Christians.

Paul did not found the Church at Rome. In fact, he had never visited Rome before he wrote his letter to the Romans. The Church at Rome emerged first (and probably quite early) out of the large Jewish population there. By the time Paul wrote to the Romans, the Church was a mixed group, with a Gentile Christian majority. Between the founding of the Church at Rome by Jews (thirties) and Paul's letter (A.D. 56–57) addressed most directly to the Gentile-Christian majority, the emperor Claudius in A.D. 49 had expelled the Jews (including Jewish Christians) from Rome (see Acts 18:2). Between the expulsion of the Jews (A.D. 49) and their return (A.D. 54), Gentiles "ran" the Church at Rome. When the Jewish Christians returned, it was only natural that there would be tensions between Gentile Christians and Jewish Christians.

These tensions probably form the background of Paul's advice to the "weak" and the "strong" in Romans 14–15. If Romans 16:1-23 was part of Paul's original letter, then Paul may have received information about the problems of the Roman Church from his network of friends and co-workers at Rome. Thus, in an act of apostolic boldness, Paul intervened in a local dispute by way of a letter. Paul's intervention, however, is not based on his own authority as an apostle. Rather, his appeal is to the authority of the gospel.

In his salutation, Paul defines the gospel: "his Son, who was descended from David according to the flesh and was declared to be Son of God with power according to the spirit of holiness by resurrection from the dead, Jesus Christ our Lord" (Rom 1:3-4). In his thesis statement (1:16-17), Paul declares the gospel to be "the power of God for salvation" and the revelation of "the righteousness of God." The gospel is available to all by faith. The old order of salvation history "to the Jew first and also to the Greek" is acknowledged, but both Jew and Greek must have faith. While recognizing the historical and ethnic differences among the Christians at Rome, Paul insists that something more fundamental binds them together and makes them equal before God—faith after the pattern of Abraham.

Much of what Paul says in Romans presupposes the modified dualism of Jewish apocalypticism. On the one hand, the children of light follow the Prince of Light and do the deeds of light. On the other hand, the children of darkness follow the Prince of Darkness and do the deeds of darkness. The Creator allows human history to continue along this way. But at some time in the future, God will put an end to darkness and leave only the kingdom of light.[1]

In the Christian translation of this apocalyptic schema, the Prince of Light is Christ. Moreover, his death and resurrection constituted the inauguration of the end-time events. Those who follow Christ do so by faith—whether they be Jews or Gentiles. They not only share his leadership, but also anticipate as "down-payment" or "first-fruits" the benefits of the fullness of God's kingdom. God's last judgment (at which his righteousness will be manifest to all) has been anticipated in the death and resurrection of Jesus. Thus, the reign of sin and death has been broken, and life in the Spirit is accessible for all—Jew and Gentile alike.

---

[1] The major text is *Manual of Discipline* 3–4. This text is from the Qumran community Rule, and is part of the group's ideology.

This fundamental thesis governs the structure of Romans. Paul first shows that all people—Gentiles and Jews—need the revelation of God's righteousness in Christ (1:18–3:20). Next, he explains how faith, exemplified by Abraham, is the entry point into God's righteousness (3:21–4:25). Then, he reflects on how Christ has broken the power of sin, death, and the Law (5:1–7:25) and freed both Jews and Gentiles for life in the Spirit (8:1-39). Next, Paul has to deal with a painful and embarrassing fact: Not all Jews have accepted the gospel. How is Paul to explain the present disinterest of many Jews in the gospel? How does this fit with God's promises to Israel? What will become of unbelieving Israel? These topics are treated in chapters 9–11. Finally, in chapters 12-15, Paul makes suggestions about the bearing of God's righteousness on everyday Christian life.

The Plight of Jews Apart from Christ (2:1-3:20)

In the letters treated thus far, Paul had been talking directly about Jewish Christians and their kind of Christianity, and only obliquely about non-Christian Jews. In Romans, however, Paul addresses directly the plight of Jews before and apart from Christ. Their plight, according to Paul, was that they were under the dominion of sin and death (the Pauline interpretation of the reign of the apocalyptic Angel of Darkness). Jews needed the revelation of God's righteousness in Christ every bit as much as Gentiles did.

That the Gentiles needed the revelation of God's righteousness in Christ is explained in Romans 1:18-32. The Gentiles had the opportunity to know God from creation: "For what can be known about God is plain to them, because God has shown it to them" (1:19). Instead of accepting this natural knowledge of God and living by it, they refused to honor God and involved themselves in a downward spiral of idolatry, impurity, and other vices. Their fundamental mistake about God and their preference for gods of their own making led them to the point where they deserved God's condemnation. The Gentiles, so enmeshed in the cycle of evil, clearly needed an intervention from God.

Many Jews would have agreed with Paul's negative assessment of contemporary paganism. The startling feature of Paul's argument was his contention that Jews also needed the revelation of God's righteousness in Christ. After all, Jews know God not only from nature and creation, but especially from the Torah. The Torah provides the authoritative guidance to know God's will. What more did Jews need before and apart from Christ?

Paul's indictment of his fellow Jews is that by their actions, they, too, have fallen under the power of sin and death. In Romans 2:1-16, Paul takes to task "you who judge" for doing the very things that they condemn others for doing. Though some argue that Paul's indictment of Jews begins only in 2:17, it seems to most interpreters that those "who judge" are Jews. The background of Paul's indictment is the presumption that is stated in Wisdom 15:2: "For even if we sin, we are yours." In Paul's view, knowledge of God's will in the Torah has not stopped Israel from sinning: "you, the judge, are doing the very same things [as the Gentiles do]" (Rom 2:1). It will not protect Israel from God's judgment either: "But by your hard and impenitent heart, you are storing up wrath for yourself on the day of wrath, when God's righteous judgment will be revealed" (2:5).

Though Paul continues to respect the order of salvation history ("the Jew first and also the Greek," 2:10), he insists that each will be judged according to one's deeds (2:6) and that "God shows no partiality" (2:11). Thus, God's wrath and fury as well as anguish and distress remain real possibilities for both Jews and Gentiles. Belonging to Israel and having the Torah are no guarantees of eternal life. All they mean is that Jews will be judged according to different criteria: "All who have sinned under the Law will be judged by the Law" (2:12).

In 2:17-24, Paul makes the point that Jews do the very things that the Law condemns. First, he acknowledges the prerogatives of Israel ("a guide to the blind, a light to those in darkness, a corrector of the foolish, a teacher of children, having in the Law the embodiment of knowledge and truth . . .," 2:19-20). Then, he accuses Jews of not practicing what they preach. Rather, Jews steal, commit adultery, rob temples, and break the Law (2:21-23). He clinches his argument by quoting Isaiah 52:5: "The name of God is blasphemed among the Gentiles because of you" (Rom 2:24).

At two points (2:13-16; 2:25-29), Paul interrupts his indictment of fellow Jews to spiritualize and thus redefine Law-observance and circumcision. In 2:13-16, Paul paints the verbal picture of Gentiles who "do instinctively what the Law requires" and thus are "a law to themselves." In 2:25-29, Paul asserts that true circumcision is not "something external and physical," but rather "a matter of the heart . . . spiritual and not literal." Paul even plays with what it means to be a Jew: "a person is a Jew who is one inwardly" (2:29).

Just as Paul seems to be moving toward separating the Law, circumcision, and even Jewish identity from historic Israel, he raises an obvious and important question: "Then what advantage has the Jew?" (3:1). He only begins to answer: "They were entrusted with the oracles of God" (3:2). The next question (3:3) concerns the unfaithfulness of historic Israel: That will not cancel the faithfulness of God. These two questions anticipate Paul's major concerns in Romans 9–11: the privileges of Israel, and the faithfulness of God in relation to Israel's unfaithfulness.

Paul holds on to a place for Israel in salvation history ("the Jew first"). It retains its historic privileges (see 9:4-5). His point in 2:1–3:20 is that "all, both Jews and Greeks, are under the power of sin" (3:9), and therefore in need of the revelation of God's righteousness in Christ. To confirm his judgment that even Jews are "under the power of sin," Paul in 3:10-18 weaves a series of isolated biblical texts to "prove" that every Jew in every bodily part is not righteous before God, and thus is as badly off as the Gentiles are. Thus, the Law itself convicts its alleged adherents.

Why then the Law? At the end of 3:20, Paul introduces a theme to be developed in chapters 4–8: "through the Law comes the knowledge of sin." The Law defines, objectifies, and codifies sinful behavior. It thus serves even as a stimulus to sin, because it puts ideas into people's heads about what constitutes sinful behavior. This assessment of the Law puts it on the "wrong" side and makes it a tool and ally of sin and death.

Where do Jews stand apart from Christ? What is their plight? They remain God's special people, because they have been entrusted with God's oracles (the Scriptures, especially as these point to Christ). Yet in practice, they stand in as much need of the revelation of God's righteousness as the pagans do. They have the Torah as the guide to God's will. And yet, they refuse the Law's guidance and sin as the Gentiles do. Indeed, some pagans seem to be better at doing God's will than Jews are, and so Paul flirts with redefining the observance of the Law, circumcision, and Jewish identity.

Thus, the plight of Jews apart from Christ is the same as that of pagans: "all, both Jews and Greeks, are under the power of sin" (3:9). Even the Law, because it brings "knowledge of sin," seems to be on the side of sin and death against Christ and God's righteousness. Notice that at the outset, Paul talked about the Law in a positive way ("the embodiment of knowledge and truth" 2:20). But by the end, it is the ally of sin.

Christ the Solution (3:21–8:39)

Paul has carefully shown that all people—Jews and Gentiles alike—stood in need of God's righteousness revealed in Christ. In the central part of his letter to the Romans, Paul reflects on how Christ has freed Jews and Gentiles alike from the servitude imposed by sin and death (and their ally, the Law) and freed them to live life in the Spirit.

What Christ has accomplished for humans is stated at many points. One example comes in Paul's transitional statement near the end of chapter 3: "Since all have sinned and fall short of the glory of God; they are now justified by his grace as a gift, through the redemption that is in Christ Jesus" (3:23-24). In Christ, the last judgment has been anticipated, and now it is possible to live as having been placed by God's grace in right relationship with God: "Therefore, since we are justified by faith, we have peace with God through our Lord Jesus Christ" (5:1). What made this new relationship possible was the death of Christ: "while we were still sinners, Christ died for us" (5:8). Now it is possible to escape the fate visited upon humankind through Adam's sin and enjoy the benefits of the justification brought about by Christ (5:12-21). Now it is possible to leave the sphere of the flesh, and of sin and death, and of the Law in order to live the life of the Spirit: "But you are not in the flesh; you are in the Spirit, since the Spirit of God dwells in you" (8:9).

Where does all this leave the Jew who does not profess faith in Christ? Where does this leave one who takes the Torah as the guide in the present rather than Christ? According to Paul, such Jews are on the wrong track. In Romans 4, Paul goes over much the same ground that he did in Galatians 3 with regard to Abraham. He presents Abraham as the model of faith: "Abraham believed God, and it was reckoned to him as righteousness" (Rom 4:3; see Gen 15:6). Then, he separates Abraham's faith and God's declaration of his righteousness from circumcision and the Law. Circumcision came later (Gen 17), and the Law "brings wrath" (that is, its infringement results in condemnation at God's judgment). Paul, of course, in Romans 4 is addressing Gentile Christians primarily and explaining why they do not have to undergo circumcision or obey the Torah completely. But what Paul says to them suggests that Jews who imagine that circumcision and Torah-observance constitute the correct way to God are mistaken.

With Christ, the reign of sin and death has been effectively broken. Therefore, in Paul's estimation, "we are not under law (= the Law) but under grace" (6:15). In 7:1-3, Paul uses the analogy of a married woman who, while her husband lives, is not free to marry someone else, but is free once her husband dies. The point is that with Christ, "you have died to the Law" (7:4) and are no longer slaves to sin and death, and therefore are free to live "in the new life of the Spirit" (7:6).

Romans 7:7-25 is one of the most fascinating and controversial texts in the New Testament. In it, Paul uses first-person language ("I") to describe the anguish of a person who struggles to be free of sin and the Law but cannot seem to succeed. The passage is often assumed to be Paul's autobiography and, therefore, testimony to his guilty conscience. But elsewhere (Phil 3:6), he declares himself to have been "as to righteousness under the Law, blameless." Nor does it seem to fit with what Paul describes as being his present state as a Christian. The best way to take Romans 7:7-25 is as Paul's description of a typical life under sin and the Law. Insofar as Paul shared that way of life before his experience of Christ, the text is autobiographical—but only in that secondary way. Paul wants to picture life before and apart from Christ in Romans 7.

That life emerges as a complex and painful interaction between sin and the Law. Though Paul affirms that the Law is "holy and just and good" (7:12) and even "spiritual" (7:14) in the sense that it belongs with the Spirit rather than the "flesh," nevertheless, in practice, it functions as an ally of sin because it gives knowledge of sin (7:7) and even gives life to sin (7:8-11). Thus, persons apart from Christ find themselves torn by forces warring within themselves: "With my mind, I am a slave to the law of God, but with my flesh, I am a slave to the law of sin" (7:25). Those who follow the Law, as Paul did, end up in this terrible tension whereby they become a kind of battleground for sin and the Law to play out their deadly drama.

Why then the Law? In Romans, Paul makes both positive and negative statements about the Law. On the positive side, the Law is "holy and just and good" (7:12). It is a witness to Christ (3:21). It is spiritual (7:14); that is, it belongs with the spirit/Holy Spirit. On the negative side, the Law brings knowledge of sin (3:20; 7:7) and serves as a stimulus to sin (7:8-11). In practice, the Law is the ally of sin and death.

Paul contends that Christians are not under the Law (6:14-15). Nevertheless, he also claims that Christians "uphold the Law" (3:31), and that "the just requirement of the Law" is fulfilled in them (8:4). As in Galatians, Paul appears to accept the salvation-historical function of the Law while rejecting the idea that it retains existential significance for Christians. Though mainly addressing Gentile Christians on these matters, Paul would appear to be led by his own logic to conclude that the Law has no real significance for Jewish Christians either.

The Mystery of Israel (9–11)

In Romans 2-3, Paul described Israel before and apart from Christ. He showed that Jews, like pagans, needed the revelation of God's righteousness in Christ. But what about Israel now that God's righteousness has been revealed in Christ? Why has not all Israel accepted that revelation? By what right do Gentiles come to be part of God's people? What is the status of Jewish Christians?

When Paul takes up the "mystery" of Israel in Romans 9-11, he is not embarking on an excursus or a distraction. Rather, he is taking up issues that have been raised throughout chapters 1–8 and demand a more extensive and systematic treatment. The "mystery" of Israel involves not only non-Christian Jews, but also Jewish Christians and Gentile Christians. It concerns how these three entities fit together.

Romans 9–11 is among the most difficult and complicated texts in the New Testament. One always runs the risk of getting lost in its fascinating details. Here, however, the focus has to be the basic points that Paul made in developing his interpretation of the mystery of Israel.

Paul first (in 9:1-5) expresses his great sorrow that not all his fellow Jews have accepted the gospel. He still regards them as "my own people, my kindred according to the flesh" (9:3). And he still recognizes the privileges granted by God to Israel as the chosen people: "the adoption, the glory, the covenants, the giving of the law, the worship, and the promises . . . the patriarchs . . . the Messiah" (9:4-5). In 11:29, Paul will declare these privileges to be "irrevocable." So, Paul recognizes the continuing existence and election of Israel, and regards himself as still part of it. By becoming a Christian, Paul did not leave Israel (at least in his interpretation). Nor did the coming of Christ end the privileged status of Israel (including those who refused the gospel).

In 9:6-29, Paul deals with the question raised by Gentile acceptance and Jewish rejection of the gospel: Has the word of God failed? By "word of God," Paul refers to God's promises to Israel in the Scriptures. What Paul sets out to do is to show that Gentile acceptance and Jewish rejection are "according to the Scriptures."

Before moving into his scriptural argument, Paul makes another attempt at redefinition: "Not all Israelites truly belong to Israel, and not all of Abraham's children are his true descendants" (9:6-7). This redefinition allows Paul to explain why some Jews and Gentiles are "in" and some other Jews are "out." By a series of scriptural quotations (Gen 21:12; 18:10, 14; 25:23; Mal 1:2-3) concerning the patriarchs, Paul shows that mere physical origin does not determine one's status in the children of Abraham. Even in the case of the twins, Jacob and Esau, God acted with sovereign freedom in loving one and hating the other. Likewise, in Romans 9:14-23, Paul gives another example of the free power of God: Moses and Pharaoh (see Exod 33:19; 9:16; 4:21).

The principle here is God's freedom in election, with "predestination" at best a corollary to which Paul gave little thought: "he has mercy on whomever he chooses, and he hardens the heart of whomever he chooses" (Rom 9:18). For humans to object to God's exercise of sovereign freedom is like the lump of clay giving orders to the potter (9:19-23).

Before pursuing the theme of Israel's (partial) rejection of the gospel, Paul establishes that the present but provisional goal of God's plan is the Church made up of Gentile and Jewish Christians. He appeals to Hosea 2:25 (23) and 2:1 (1:10) to show that the Gentiles ("not my people . . . not beloved") can be called "children of the living God" (Rom 9:25-26). He appeals to Isaiah 10:22-23 and 1:9 to establish the Jewish Christians as the "remnant" of Israel and thus the means by which Israel's identity as bearer of the promises to Abraham is kept alive (Rom 9:27-29).

Thus far in 9:1-29, Paul has acknowledged the salvation-historical privileges of Israel and his own place within Israel. He has distinguished three groups: the Jewish-Christian remnant, the Gentile Christians, and other Jews. In chapters 1–8, he has explained how Gentiles can be part of God's people. What he needs now to explain and interpret is the painful fact that not all Israel has responded to the gospel as Paul did. Does God have a purpose in allowing part of Israel to reject the gospel?

The present but provisional state of salvation history according to Paul means that some Jews find themselves on the "wrong way." That wrong way is striving for "righteousness that is based on the Law . . . as if it were based on works" (9:31-32). According to Paul, Jews of his day imagined that by careful observance of the Torah, they could achieve righteousness before God. Most of the Jewish literature from the period presents good conduct according to God's Law as the fitting response to God's prior revelation and election. There is some controversy as to where Paul got his idea of righteousness by works. Does it reflect his own experience and that of other Jews? If so, it is an understandable but, nevertheless, perverse reading of the Torah. Or is Paul so convinced that Christ is the way to God now that any proposal of a rival way is caricatured and refuted? Wherever Paul got the idea, whether it is the product of his experience or his imagination, the result has been the stereotype of legalism applied to Jews by Christians and (in pre-ecumenical times) to Catholics by Protestants.

Paul begins his reflection on the "two ways" (9:30–10:21) by a paradoxical contrast reminiscent of 2:14-16: Gentiles who historically have not pursued righteousness have attained it through faith, whereas Israel which historically has pursued righteousness does not succeed—because it acts as if righteousness were based on works (9:30-32). For the latter, Christ becomes a stumbling block (9:33 = Isa 28:16; 8:14). This same contrast between the way of faith and the way of the Law has already appeared in Galatians 3–4, 2 Corinthians 3, and Romans 4.

Given Paul's analysis of the "two ways," where does this leave non-Christian Jews? In ignorance, according to Paul, because they fail to understand the nature of God's righteousness (it is by God's grace and demands faith in response) and seek to substitute for it their own brand of righteousness. Paul protests his continuing affection for his fellow Jews ("my heart's desire and prayer to God for them is that they may be saved," 10:1). He admits their sincerity ("they have a zeal for God," 10:2). But from Paul's theological perspective, their zeal is "not enlightened."

Paul's fellow Jews have failed to recognize that Christ is the "end" of the Law. The Greek word for "end" (*telos*) carries the same ambiguity as the English word does: It can mean "goal" (the end for which the activity is undertaken and toward which it tends) and "termination" (something ceases to exist). Paul's primary meaning is most likely "goal": Christ is that to which the Law points, and he is its fulfillment. The Law does not cease to exist, though it does cease to exist as a principle of salvation (although it never really was one, in Paul's judgment). Now that Christ has come and the Law has reached its goal, God's righteousness is available to all people—"for everyone who believes" (10:4).

The "two ways" use different media. The "righteousness that comes from the Law" (10:5) is written in the Law of Moses. Its adherents must live by what is written there. The "righteousness that comes from faith" (10:6) is present in the word of Christian teaching: "The word is near you, on your lips and in your heart" (10:8 = Deut 30:14). What that word requires is belief in ("in your heart") and confession of ("on your lips") the resurrection of

Jesus. It is available to all people, "for there is no distinction between Jew and Greek" (10:12).

Having established the preached word of the gospel as the proper medium of the righteousness that comes from faith, Paul in 10:14-21 argues that his fellow Jews should have accepted that word. They cannot plead that the gospel was never made available to them. In 10:14-17, Paul outlines (but in reverse) the process of evangelization: The apostle is sent; the gospel is preached; the word is heard; people believe; and believers call upon the Lord. Then, in 10:18-21, Paul uses biblical quotations to show that Israel has heard the gospel (Ps 19:5) and failed to grasp the real significance of the Gentile acceptance of the gospel (Deut 32:21; Isa 65:1). Therefore, in the words of Isa 65:2, they remain "a disobedient and contrary people."

Thus far, Paul has been contrasting the "two ways": the righteousness that comes from the Law, and the righteousness that comes from faith. He is convinced that the former way is wrong and that its adherents are mistaken. His conviction arose from his own experience and that of the Gentile Christians to whom his ministry was devoted. Where does this conviction leave Paul's fellow Jews who have not accepted the gospel? His judgment against them in Romans 10:18-21 seems devastating: "a disobedient and contrary people."

Nevertheless, Paul does not give up on his fellow Jews. And the basic reasons for Paul's hope for "all Israel" are buried in two of the Scripture texts that Paul uses against his fellow Jews. In 10:19, Paul quotes Deuteronomy 32:21 and identifies "not a nation" and "a foolish nation" as the Gentiles. Most readers glide over the introductory phrase: "I (God) will make you (Israel) jealous. . . ." In Romans 11, Paul will interpret Gentile acceptance of the gospel as a divine, providential strategy to bring all Israel to the gospel. In 10:21, Paul quotes Isaiah 65:2 to condemn unbelieving Israel as "a disobedient and contrary people." Yet that verse begins with God's promise of continuing love for Israel: "All day long, I have held out my hands." The themes of providential jealousy and divine fidelity are essential elements in Paul's vision of a reunited people of God.

In 11:1, Paul poses the question that has been on his mind since the beginning of Romans 9: "Has God rejected his people?" His answer is "No!" He first points to himself as a Jewish Christian ("an Israelite, a descendant of Abraham, a member of the tribe of Benjamin," 9:1) as living proof. And then, in 11:2-6, he appeals to the remnant in Israel represented by Elijah and the 7,000 who refused to worship Baal (1 Kgs 18–19) as scriptural precedent for the remnant formed by the Jewish Christians. Thus, the Jewish-Christian remnant proves that God has not rejected his people.

But what about other Jews? Has God rejected those outside the Jewish-Christian remnant? Paul begins his evaluation of them (which he will complete in Romans 11:25-32) by introducing the image of "hardening" ("the rest were hardened," 11:7). What that image means is expanded in 11:8-10 by several other images in biblical quotations, first from Deuteronomy 29:3/Isaiah 6:9-10 ("eyes that would not see and ears that would not hear") and then from Psalm 69:23-24 ("let their eyes be darkened . . . their backs forever bent"). The passive verbs suggest that God is the agent of the hardening, or at least God allows it. The providential purpose of the hardening will be explained in what follows in Romans 11.

The theme of "jealousy" raised first in 10:19 is developed in 11:11-15. Paul thought that he could discern the rationale of the divine plan. The "hardening" of part of Israel is only temporary. The success of the Gentile mission had, as its ultimate purpose, to make "hardened" Israel jealous and eventually to lead them to accept the gospel. The obduracy of Israel drove Jewish Christians such as Paul to preach the gospel to non-Jews. Paul reasons: "If their rejection is the reconciliation of the world, what will their acceptance be but life from the dead!" (11:15). If we take seriously Paul's words "acceptance" and "life from the dead," then it would seem that the inclusion of the "hardened" part of Israel will involve the acceptance of the gospel, and that it will take place at the end of human history along with the resurrection of the dead. Thus, Paul's conviction about God's fidelity to Israel led him to see that even the "hardened" part of Israel has a present role (to be made jealous by Gentile acceptance of the gospel) and a future role in the people of God (to be united with the Jewish and Gentile Christians).

In 11:16, Paul puts forward two images that focus on the relation between the part and the whole: the first-fruits of the dough (see Num 15:20-21), and the root of the tree. The Jewish-Christian remnant represents the part (first-fruits and root) that makes holy the others (Gentiles and Jews).

Paul, in 11:17-24, develops the root-branches image with reference to the olive tree. The olive tree has a root (Israel represented by Jewish Christians), wild shoots grafted onto the tree (Gentile Christians), and branches broken off but capable of being grafted back on (other Jews). With this image, Paul affirms the continuity between the Church and Israel, reminds the Gentiles of their dependence on their Jewish roots, and holds out the hope that eventually all Israel will be reunited in the olive tree.

Paul's readers were surely familiar with olive trees, for these were widely cultivated all over the Mediterranean area. They may also have known something about the Old Testament depictions of Israel as an olive tree (see Hos 14:6; Jer 11:16). They may even have known that grafting the branches of wild olives onto an old tree served to rejuvenate the tree.[2] Thus, the grafting on of the Gentile branches has given new life to the tree. But since the process (not merely the new branches) rejuvenates the tree, the Gentiles are warned against boasting about their contribution. It is God's work.

As part of his warning against Gentile boasting, Paul looks forward in 11:23-24 to the full inclusion of "all Israel" in the olive tree. If God can graft wild olive branches (Gentiles) onto the tree, surely God can graft the natural branches back into their own olive tree. The qualifying clause "if they do not persist in unbelief" (11:23) suggests that Paul regarded faith as the prerequisite for Jewish sharing in "the rich root of the olive tree" (11:17).

Has God rejected his people? No! The Jewish Christians function as the remnant; they represent the root of the olive tree—the principle of continuity. Other Jews have been temporarily and providentially dissassociated from the olive tree. But "if they do not persist in unbelief," they, too, will be once again united with the root that carries the life of Israel.

[2]A. J. Baxter and J. A. Ziesler, "Paul and Arboriculture: Romans 11:17-24," *JSNT* 24 (1985) 25–32.

Conclusion

In formulating his gospel for the Roman Christians, Paul is forced to consider the reality of Jews who have not accepted the gospel. According to Paul, such Jews, despite the salvation-historical privileges of Israel, find themselves under the dominion of sin and death, and therefore need the revelation of God's righteousness in Christ. In the meantime, Jewish Christians and their Gentile converts represent the people of God in the present, and non-Christian Jews are pursuing the way of Torah—which does not lead to right relationship with God. The Law in itself is "holy and just and good" (7:12); it bears witness to Christ, and Christians uphold it. But when Jews try to use the Law to achieve what according to Paul only Christ could achieve, their Law becomes an ally of sin and death.

Paul seeks to situate the Jews who have not accepted the gospel with reference to Jewish Christians like himself and Gentile Christians. In the present, these other Jews are in a kind of salvation-historical "limbo": They are in ignorance, under a divinely induced "hardening," pursuing the wrong way to God, and cut off from the richness and the life that is God's olive tree, Israel. In the future, however, they will rejoin Israel "if they do not persist in unbelief" (11:23). Paul's hope for non-Christian Israel is based on his trust in God's fidelity to Israel and his interpretation that God's purpose in "hardening" some in Israel was to draw Gentiles into God's people and eventually to entice the remaining Jews through "jealousy" at the success of the Gentile mission. How all this will work out is sketched in Romans 11:25-32.

4

Romans 11:25-32

This book takes its impetus from Paul's statement in Romans 11:26a: "And so all Israel will be saved." Our first task is to understand that statement in its immediate context—in Romans 11:25-32, which is the climax of Paul's argument in chapters 9 through 11. The text, according to the New Revised Standard Version, reads as follows:

> 25. So that you may not claim to be wiser than you are, brothers and sisters, I want you to understand this mystery: a hardening has come upon part of Israel, until the full number of the Gentiles has come in.   26. And so all Israel will be saved, as it is written.
>
> "Out of Zion will come the Deliverer;
> he will banish ungodliness from Jacob."
> 27. "And this is my covenant with them,
> when I take away their sins."
>
> 28. As regards the gospel they are enemies of God for your sake, but as regards election they are beloved, for the sake of their ancestors; 29. for the gifts and the calling of God are irrevocable. 30. Just as you were once disobedient to God but have now received mercy because of their disobedience, 31. so they have now been disobedient in order that, by the mercy shown to you, they too may now receive mercy. 32. For God has imprisoned all in disobedience so that he may be merciful to all.

The first part (11:25-27) is the revelation of the "mystery" of God's plan: introduction (11:25a), the mystery (11:25b–26a), and the biblical basis (11:26b–27). The second part (11:28-32) summarizes the mystery and, indeed, the entire argument of Romans 9–11. One can divide the summary into three segments (11:28-29; 11:30-31; 11:32), though in fact such a division is a bit artificial.

The Mystery (11:25-27)

Introduction (Rom 11:25a): "So that you may not claim to be wiser than you are, brothers and sisters, I want you to understand this mystery." The persons being addressed in this entire passage ("you") are Gentile Christians at Rome, as in 11:13 ("Now I am speaking to you Gentiles"). They need to be reminded of their place in God's plan of salvation and (more importantly, here) of Israel's place within that plan as Paul interprets it. The same language is used as a general warning in Romans 12:16: "Do not claim to be wiser than you are." Both expressions echo Proverbs 3:7: "Do not be wise in your own eyes." The basic point is clear: Paul wishes to deflate the spiritual pretentiousness of the Gentile Christians at Rome by reminding them of their subordinate place in salvation history and especially of the spiritual debt that they owe to Israel.

The address "brothers" (*adelphoi*) is common in Romans (see 1:13; 7:1, 4; 8:12; 10:1; 12:1; 15:14, 30; 16:17) and other Pauline letters (1 Cor 1:10, 11, 26, etc.). The inclusive translation in the NRSV ("brothers and sisters"), though not strictly warranted by the Greek original, is an appropriate rendering not only for English idiom today, but also in view of the prominent roles played by women in the Christian community at Rome according to Romans 16:1-16.

"I want you to understand" makes into a positive statement what in Greek is expressed negatively: "I do not wish you to be ignorant (or, unaware)." Paul uses this formula to give special importance to what follows in Romans 1:13 and elsewhere (1 Cor 10:1; 12:1; 2 Cor 1:8; 1 Thess 4:13). Coupled with the direct address ("brothers and sisters"), the expression prepares for Paul's revelation of the great "mystery."

In the Greco-Roman mystery cults, a *mystērion* referred to the secret knowledge that must be kept from the uninitiated. But Paul wishes everyone to know this "mystery." The background of his expression is Jewish apocalypticism, especially the book of Daniel. There, the seer is able to interpret and explain dreams and visions precisely because God reveals their meaning to him: "He reveals deep and hidden things . . . there is a God in heaven who reveals mysteries" (Dan 2:22, 28). The same dynamic of mysteries being resolved and unveiled by God to interpreters underlies the Qumran community's "Pesharim"—in which the mysteries of the Prophets and Psalms are shown to pertain to the community's life and history.[1]

When Paul says that he has a mystery to express, he means that now the puzzle of (part of) Israel's rejection of the gospel has been solved for him. He implies that God has revealed the solution to him, and states that now he is going to share that solution with the Gentile Christians at Rome. Paul takes on the persona of Daniel and other apocalyptic visionaries. He has used several rhetorical techniques to underline the importance of what he is going to say. He has placed his statement at the end of a long and involved meditation. All is now prepared for Paul to communicate his revelation about Israel's present and future.

The Mystery (11:25b–26a): "A hardening has come upon part of Israel, until the full number of Gentiles has come in. And so all Israel will be saved." The mystery that Paul unveils has three parts, each one of which is significant in Paul's understanding of God's plan for Jews and Gentiles.

The image of "hardening" (*pōrōsis*) in the first unit picks up an image used in Rom 11:7 to describe the difference between the "elect" and "the rest" within Israel: "The elected obtained it, but the rest were hardened." The metaphor alludes to the knitting together of broken bones or the forming of a stone in the bladder. It describes obtuse people, unable to hear and understand anything new or important. There is some manuscript evidence for "blindness" (*pērōsis*) as the leading image here. In either case, the metaphor refers to obtuseness on Israel's part.

---

[1] M. P. Horgan, *Pesharim: Qumran Interpretation of Biblical Books* (Washington, D.C.: Catholic Biblical Association, 1979).

Who is the agent of this obtuseness? The impersonal way in which it is described ("has come upon") suggests divine agency: God permits or even providentially causes the hardening to come upon some in Israel. It is easy to hear in the background the providential "hardening" that God promises Isaiah as he takes up the prophetic vocation: "Go and say to this people: 'Keep listening, but do not comprehend, keep looking, but do not understand. . . .'" (Isa 6:9-10). Early Christians took up this text to explain why many Jews rejected Jesus and his gospel (see Matt 13:14-15; Mark 4:12; John 12:40; Acts 28:26-27). God allows the temporary hardening so that eventually greater good may come.[2]

The term "Israel" is a collective noun embracing both Christian Jews (like Paul) and other Jews. This usage prepares for the collective meaning of "Israel" in Romans 11:26a. The sense is national or ethnic Israel. It should not be interpreted in the light of Paul's redefinition in Romans 9:6: "For not all Israelites truly belong to Israel" (literally, "For not all those from Israel are Israel"). Rather, it should be taken with the other references to Israel in chapters 9-11 (9:27, 31; 10:19; 11:2, 7), where it occurs in a "national" sense mainly to describe those many Jews who reject the gospel. The adverbial phrase "in part" (*apo merous*) qualifies "Israel" in the collective sense: Some (even many), but not all, Jews were "hardened."

The first element in Paul's revelation of the mystery of God's plan is that God has allowed some in Israel to be obtuse with regard to the gospel. The second element concerns the Gentiles. The thrust of Paul's missionary activity and of his writing to the Romans has been to insist that through Christ, Gentiles have a right to be part of God's people along with Israel. Here he asserts that Israel's partial "hardening" (Jewish Christians are a remnant constituting the exception) is temporary ("until" = *achri hou*): It will end when "the full number of Gentiles has come in." Into what do the Gentiles come? One thinks immediately of Gospel sayings about entering God's kingdom or life (see Matt 5:20; 7:13-14, 21; 18:3; etc.), though in the present context it could be the people of God or the Church.

[2]C. A. Evans, *To See and Not Perceive. Isaiah 6:9-10 in Early Jewish and Christian Interpretation* (Sheffield, UK: JSOT Press, 1989).

The term "full number" (*plērōma*) was used by Paul previously with respect to Israel's providential "stumbling" in Romans 11:12: "How much more will their full inclusion mean!" With regard to the Gentiles, it implies the idea of a quota or fixed number that has to be reached before Israel's hardening can end. (See Rev 7:1-8 for the 144,000 "sealed out of every tribe of the people of Israel" as an example of the quota idea applied to Israel.) The concept of Gentiles' joining with Israel is prominent in Isaiah 2:2-4 and Zechariah 8:20-23. Thus, the second element in Paul's revelation looks to the future when the number of Gentiles that "has come in" reaches the quota fixed by God. This will mean the end of the hardening of part of Israel.

The third element in Paul's revelation concerns the future of "all Israel." The adverb "so" (*houtōs*) is emphatic in its position at the beginning of the unit. Its basic meaning is modal ("thus") rather than temporal ("then"), though here the two dimensions cannot be sharply separated. How will all Israel be saved? First, by God's hardening of part of Israel and then by the full inclusion of Gentiles. The passive language again suggests that the providential hand of God is behind these events.

The meaning of "all Israel" is collective, in keeping with the biblical idiom (1 Sam 7:5; 25:1; 1 Kgs 12:1; 2 Chr 12:1; and Dan 9:11). It can hardly refer to Jewish Christians only, since in the preceding verse, "Israel" clearly has a wider meaning. It can hardly refer to the Church made up of believing Jews and Gentiles, since that would be anticlimactic in Romans 11:25-26.

Granted that "all Israel" encompasses national or ethnic Israel, does it include all Jews automatically and without exception? Probably not. Mishnah *Sanhedrin*, chapter 10, begins with a general statement: "All Israel has a portion in the world to come." Then it proceeds to present a long list of those who have no share in the world to come: Those who deny the biblical basis of the doctrine of the resurrection, certain wicked kings (Jeroboam, Ahab, Manasseh), etc. The parallel is important for two reasons: It shows that "all Israel" can be used as a collective without necessarily implying the inclusion of each and every Israelite, and it ties the future of Israel in with the fullness of God's kingdom ("the world to come").

When will all Israel's salvation take place? That the event will be future from Paul's perspective is clear from the tense of the verb ("will be saved" = *sōthēsetai*). But when? Paul can use "salvation" language to describe what has already happened to people (Rom 8:24), what will happen to them if they believe (Rom 10:9, 13-14), and what will happen to them in the end of human history (Rom 5:9-10).

Paul does not give us much help in choosing here between the second and third options. The parallel with *m. Sanhedrin* 10 ("all Israel" used in an eschatological context) and the accompanying quotation of Isaiah 59:20-21; 27:9 in Romans 11:26b-27 suggest the eschatological interpretation: At the end of human history, all Israel will be saved. Nevertheless, one cannot rule out at this point the idea that Israel's salvation takes place within human history. Moreover, Paul has not told us precisely how all Israel will be saved. Is it through God's gracious action, or the missionary efforts of Christians, or through Israel's public profession of faith in Christ? These options have important consequences, as we will see.

Biblical Basis (11:26b-27):

> "Out of Zion will come the Deliverer;
> he will banish ungodliness from Jacob.
> And this is my covenant with them,
> when I take away their sins."

The biblical quotation comments on the partial hardening of Israel and the subsequent salvation of "all Israel." The first three lines are from Isaiah 59:20-21a, and the fourth line is from Isaiah 27:9. It is possible that these texts had already been combined in some kind of anthology of biblical quotations (such as have been found among the Qumran scrolls).

In Isaiah 59:20, the Deliverer is surely Yahweh. In the biblical context, no human redeemer appears in the midst of oppression and injustice among God's people: "there was no one to intervene" (59:16). Therefore, God takes up the role of Israel's Deliverer.

Who is the Deliverer in Romans 11:26b? It could be Yahweh as in Isa 59:20. Or it could be (and more likely is) Christ. The one significant difference between the Septuagint version and what appears in Romans 11:26b concerns the preposition before Zion: "for the sake of" (*heneken*) in the Septuagint, and "out of" (*ek*) in Romans. If the Deliverer is Christ and the change of preposition is deliberate, Paul seems to be thinking of the parousia or second coming of Christ (see 1 Thess 1:10), and of "Zion" as the heavenly Jerusalem (see Gal 4:26). This interpretation would confirm the eschatological character of the salvation of all Israel forecast in Romans 11:26a. It is strengthened by the rabbinic application of Isaiah 59:20 to the Messiah (*b. Sanh.* 98a). The Redeemer's task is to banish ungodliness from Jacob, in both the Septuagint and Romans; compare the Hebrew text: "he will come . . . as Redeemer to those in Jacob who turn from transgression."

In Isaiah 59:21, the Lord promises that his spirit and his words will always abide with the people. In Romans 11:27, the introduction is the same: The word "this" is emphatic and points forward to the promise; "covenant" (*diathēkē*) carries the meaning of "promise" but also conveys the solemnity associated with the biblical concept of "covenant."

The content of the promise, however, differs from that in Isaiah 59:21b: It is the forgiveness of the people's sins rather than the pledge of the abiding presence of God's word and God's spirit among them. The new promise is taken from the Septuagint of Isaiah 27:9: "when I take away his sin." The Pauline version differs from the Septuagint by reason of the plural object of the verb: "their sins." The content of the new promise is the forgiveness of Israel's sins. The combination of "covenant" (*diathēkē*) and forgiveness of sins is reminiscent of the "new covenant" promise in Jer 31:34: "I will forgive their iniquity, and remember their sins no more."

What does Paul's "scriptural proof" really prove? The combination of Isaiah 59:20b ("he will banish ungodliness from Jacob") and 27:9 ("when I take away their sins") indicates that the "salvation" of all Israel will involve the forgiveness of sins. What remains unclear is the identity of the Deliverer: God or Christ? If Christ is the Deliverer, then Israel's salvation is tied to Christ directly and is most likely to be an eschatological event (when Christ comes from the heavenly Zion). If God is the Deliverer (as in Isaiah), then there is not a necessary connection between Christ and Israel's salvation; and one can talk legitimately of God's own way of salvation for Israel. Paul's use of Scripture elsewhere and the logic of his argument throughout Romans suggest the Christological interpretation. But it is by no means certain.

Summaries 11:28-32

Summary No. 1 (11:28-29): "As regards the gospel, they are enemies [of God] for your sake; but as regards election, they are beloved, for the sake of their ancestors; for the gifts and the calling of God are irrevocable." These verses pick up on the "hardening" of part of Israel from the preceding verses and also begin Paul's summary or recapitulation of his whole argument in chapters 9-11. The "they" in 11:28 refers to that part of Israel that has been hardened and has not accepted the gospel. The "gospel" has already been defined in Romans 1:3-4 ("his Son, who was descended from David . . ."). Whether "enemies" (*echthroi*) should be taken actively or passively is not clear, though the adjective in the second member ("beloved") suggests a passive sense. The NRSV (following the RSV) makes them into "enemies of God" for no good textual reason, since they are really opposed to the spread of the gospel. As was the case with the providential hardening that came on part of Israel, the opposition of unbelieving Israel to the spread of the gospel has been permitted for the benefit of the Gentile Christians ("for your sake"). Thus, the first member of Romans 11:28 summarizes what Paul said in 11:11-14 ("their defeat means riches for Gentiles").

The second member of Rom 11:28 follows the structure of the first member. Israel remains "beloved" (*agapētoi*) because of God's choice of it as a people. The expression "for the sake of their ancestors" (literally, "fathers") probably does not allude to the rabbinic doctrine of the "merits of the fathers" according to which the deeds of Abraham, Isaac, Jacob, etc. would benefit the later generations of Israel.[3] Rather, it is more a reminder of

---

[3]S. Schechter, *Aspects of Rabbinic Theology* (New York: Schocken, 1961) 170-98.

the early history of Israel as a chosen people. The second member of 11:28 reaffirms God's choice of Israel as a people special to God.

The nature and content of Israel's election is spelled out in 11:29. The "irrevocable" character of that election is emphasized by the position of the term *ametameleta* (see also 2 Cor 7:10) as the very first word. What will not be taken back are God's "gifts" to Israel. These "gifts" (*charismata*) include at least what were listed in Romans 9:4-5: "the adoption, the glory, the covenants, the giving of the Law, the worship, and the promises . . . the patriarchs . . . the Messiah." How precisely God's "calling" relates to the "gifts" (a mere synonym, a reference to the process outlined in 9:6-29, an additional gift or a particularization of the gifts?) is not clear. What is clear, however, is Paul's endorsement of the continuing nature of God's election of Israel, even of those Israelites who have refused to accept the gospel.

Summary No. 2 (11:30-31): "Just as you were once disobedient to God but have now received mercy because of their disobedience, so they have now been disobedient in order that by the mercy shown to you, they too may [now] receive mercy." Paul's fondness for parallel statements shown in 11:28 is even stronger in 11:30-31. The "you" are the Gentile Christians, and "they" are non-Christian Jews. After reminding the Gentile Christians of their past disobedience to God, Paul raises again the idea of a causal connection between Jewish rejection of the gospel and Gentile acceptance of it that he developed in the earlier parts of chapter 11 ("their stumbling means riches for the world" [11:12]; "their rejection is the reconciliation of the world" [11:15]). But Paul finds a providential reason in Israel's stumbling and rejection. Its disobedience will be the occasion for another display of mercy on God's part, this time to unbelieving Israel. As Paul suggested in 11:11, 14, God's purpose in having the Gentiles accept the gospel is to induce Jews to accept it also. Thus, all peoples— Jews and Gentiles alike—will be the recipients of God's saving mercy.

In 11:31, the word "now" (*nun*) appears twice. The first occurrence ("they have now been disobedient") causes no problem. But the second "now" ("they too may [now] receive mercy") does present a problem. Does Paul mean to say that the process of

God's showing mercy to unbelieving Israel is already going on "now?" Or is it future, as 11:26a indicated? Many important and ancient manuscripts do not have the second "now." A few manuscripts substitute the adverb "later" (*hysteron*). Some modern commentators find in the presence of the second "now" a proof that Paul thought that he lived in the last days. Others find in it the basis of a full-scale mission to the Jews in the present. It is probably best to omit the second "now" and so follow the lead of the early textual witnesses.[4] From Paul's perspective, God's display of mercy to unbelieving Israel remained in the future.

Summary No. 3 (11:32): "For God has imprisoned all in disobedience so that he may be merciful to all." The "all" refers to Jews and Gentiles alike. There is manuscript evidence for "all things" (*ta panta*) rather than "all persons" (*tous pantas*) in the first instance. But that variant may be due to Galatians 3:22: "the scripture has imprisoned all things under the power of sin." If we grant that Paul wrote "all (persons)," then Romans 11:32a is a good summary of the first major part of the letter (1:18–3:20), in which Paul tried to show that both Gentiles and Jews needed the manifestation of God's righteousness in Christ. Likewise, the second part of the verse (11:32b) is a short version of what Paul said were the consequences of Christ's death and resurrection in 3:21–8:39, especially in 3:25 ("whom God put forward as a sacrifice of atonement by his blood") with its allusion to the "mercy-seat" (see Lev 16:13-15). As in Romans 11:25-26 and 11:31, Paul finds a positive and providential divine purpose at work in God's confining all in disobedience.

Conclusion

In Romans 11:25-28, Paul reminds Gentile Christians of their place within salvation history. He explains to them that the present obduracy of part of Israel is allowed by God so that non-Jews might "come in." When the "full number" of Gentiles has been reached, all Israel will be saved. According to Isaiah 59:20-21a

[4]B. M. Metzger, *A Textual Commentary on the Greek New Testament* (London-New York: United Bible Societies, 1971) 527.

and 27:9, Israel's deliverance will be accompanied by the forgiveness of its sins. Paul is certain (by way of revelation) that God's plan is unfolding according to these three steps: partial hardening of Israel, entrance of the Gentiles, and salvation of all Israel. Paul does not tell us clearly whether all Israel's salvation will take place at the end of history (eschatological) or within history (historical). Nor does he tell us directly whether the primary agent in saving all Israel is God (theological) or Christ (Christological).

In Romans 11:29-32, Paul recapitulates not only the "mystery" revealed in 11:25b-26, but also his argument in chapters 9-11. He acknowledges the resistance of (part of) Israel to the gospel: "enemies for your sake . . . they have now been disobedient . . . all in disobedience." He maintains that Israel's present disobedience is providential: "for your sake . . . you received mercy because of their disobedience . . . so that he may be merciful." He insists that Israel's present disobedience does not nullify its status as God's chosen people: "they are beloved . . . irrevocable." Paul foresees God's plan as leading to the salvation of all Israel: "they too may [now] receive mercy . . . so that he may be merciful to all." According to Paul, Israel has a glorious future. Even its present resistance to the gospel is part of God's providential design.

There is no good reason to regard Romans 11:25-32 or all of Romans 9-11 as a later addition, or a separate piece, or an odd block, or an excursus.[5] In general, its theology flows out of and is consistent with what Paul had developed so carefully in chapters 1-8. Its apparent strangeness at some points stems from the fact that Paul here deals with an issue that he had not previously treated in a sustained way: the present and future status of those Jews who have not accepted the gospel. Paul's more than ordinary reliance on "proofs" from biblical texts and the artificiality of some of his arguments can be explained by the nature of his topic (as in Galatians 3) and the impression that he wants to leave on his readers (that he is well versed in Jewish Scripture and exegesis).

Paul's treatment of the "mystery" of God's plan of salvation in Romans 11:25-32 provides a window onto his vision of the

---

[5]F. Refoulé, "Unité de l'Épître aux Romains et histoire du salut," *Revue des Sciences Philosophiques et Théologiques* 71 (1987) 219-42.

Church. Paul could not imagine the Church without a relation to Israel. Its root is Israel, represented by Jewish Christians like himself. By God's grace, Gentiles have been grafted onto the olive tree, and there is hope that eventually other Jews will be brought back onto the olive tree also. Paul acknowledges straightforwardly the Jewishness of Jesus and his ministry to Israel: "Christ has become a servant of the circumcised" (Rom 15:8). His vision of the Church is one of Gentiles and Jews united in praising the God of Israel: "Rejoice, O Gentiles, with his [= God's] people" (Rom 15:10 = Deut 32:43 LXX).

Despite the grandeur and freshness of Paul's vision of the Church, even his enthusiastic supporters must acknowledge the limits of what Paul says. His metaphor of the olive tree leaves those Jews who do not accept the gospel in a kind of theological "no man's land" or "limbo." They will become theologically significant again only when God grafts them back onto the olive tree (= the people of God). In the meantime, in Paul's view, they continue to follow the wrong way (that of Torah) and continue to live under the dominion of sin and death.

As to when and how "all Israel will be saved," Paul is not explicit. The context, however, suggests that the salvation of all Israel will be eschatological—part of the end-time events along with the general resurrection, the parousia of Christ, and the last judgment. But did Paul really expect that 1,950 years would pass between his writing to the Romans and the occurrence of these end-time events? Romans 13:12 ("the night is far gone, the day is near") suggests otherwise.

The argument that Paul so carefully constructed in chapters 1–8 implies that the salvation of all Israel must have some connection with Christ and with faith. The logic of Romans demands the Christological interpretation of Israel's salvation. For Paul to assume that God has another, separate way for Israel (the way of Torah) would be to tear down the very case that he built up. Thus, the theological interpretation, as attractive as it might seem to people in the late twentieth century, does not correspond very well with what Paul taught. The Christological interpretation seems more appropriate.

Paul's reflection on the present and future of Jews who had not accepted the gospel in Romans 9–11 is the earliest extant attempt by a Christian to think through this difficult theological issue. Paul is trying to fit together several theological truths: God's promises to and election of Israel, Christ as the solution to humankind's plight, and the gospel's acceptance by Gentiles and rejection by many Jews. Readers today are likely to find his appeal to God's providential use of Israel's jealousy engendered by Gentile acceptance of the gospel to be artificial. They may also wonder how soon Paul thought that the eschaton would come and how applicable Paul's teaching is for a Church now deeply immersed in history for almost two thousand years.

The experimental and ambivalent nature of Paul's understanding can be sensed even in what he says about his fellow Jews in Romans 11. If the Jewish Christians, like Paul, constitute the remnant as Elijah and the seven thousand faithful Israelites did, then other Jews stand with those in Israel who worshipped Baal. Whereas the elect (Jewish Christians) obtained God's righteousness, "the rest were hardened" (11:7). Jews who have not accepted the gospel have been broken off from the olive tree that is Israel (11:17) and now function as enemies of the gospel (11:28). On the other hand, Paul insists that God still loves these non-Christian Jews and that God's gifts and calling to Israel remain irrevocable (11:28-29).

Paul's revelation of the "mystery" of salvation is not the last word on Jews in the present and future. In fact, it is the first word, the earliest substantive treatment of the topic in Scripture. Paul, however, was thoroughly convinced that he had seen something very important. And so he concluded: "O the depth of the riches and wisdom and knowledge of God!" (Rom 11:33). We should be grateful for what Paul has given us without turning his statements into "the last word."

5

Modern Scholarship

Paul's attitudes toward Judaism and its Law have been lively topics for scholarly debate in recent years.[1] Five major questions have dominated the discussions: In what sense can Paul be called a convert? What audience was Paul addressing in his letters, and what did he expect them to do vis-à-vis Judaism and the Law? What stance did Paul take regarding the Law? Was Paul consistent in his statements about the Law? What kind of future does Israel have?

What follows is not a comprehensive survey of scholarship. Neither is it a critical engagement of the leading figures in the debate. Rather, it intends to be a mainly positive presentation of the issues from the texts studied in the preceding chapters and from the contributions of modern scholars. I want to show some gains and problems for understanding Paul and Judaism from the works of contemporary students of Paul. I do not agree with everything they say, and they do not necessarily agree with one another. But when I express disagreement in this chapter, I seek only to highlight a point or to show that a particular approach goes too far or goes nowhere, not to provide a thorough assessment.

---

[1]S. Westerholm, *Israel's Law and the Church's Faith. Paul and His Recent Interpreters* (Grand Rapids: Eerdmans, 1988).

Paul the Convert

Was Paul a convert? If so, from what to what? The answers to these questions depend to a large extent on what one means by conversion and who is observing Paul.

If conversion means changing religions, moving from one religion to another, then Paul was not a convert. This is so because, in Paul's day, Judaism and Christianity were not yet viewed as separate religions. In the fifties of the first century A.D., people still looked on Christians as a peculiar kind of Jew. This was the perspective not only of outside observers, but also inside participants like Paul. Paul regarded his Christianity as the fullness of his Judaism, as the kind of Judaism that God had finally revealed in Jesus of Nazareth, not as an alternate religion.

If Paul thought that he remained within Judaism, in what did his "conversion" consist? Paul's conversion was really a move from Pharisaic Judaism to Christian Judaism, from one type of Judaism to another. Paul himself claims to have been a Pharisee (Phil 3:5). Likewise, the Lukan Paul claims to have been a Pharisee (Acts 23:6; 26:5; see 5:34).[2] There is no good reason to reject these claims.[3] But after and because of his experience of Christ, Paul regarded his efforts at living Judaism as a Pharisee to have been "loss" (Phil 3:7-8). He found a better way—"conformation" ("being formed") with Christ. Everything else had to be fitted in with that overpowering experience,

Alan F. Segal, in *Paul the Convert: The Apostolate and Apostasy of Saul the Pharisee* (New Haven: Yale University Press, 1990), describes what happened to Paul as a true conversion and specifies it as a transformation from Pharisaism to Christianity. This is where the perspective of the observer comes in. In Paul's own mind, Paul remained within Judaism. He was promoting a new, fuller kind of Judaism. But to some other Jews and even to some other Jewish Christians, Paul was going beyond the bounds of Judaism. To them, Paul looked like an apostate from Judaism. Paul's insistence on "conformation" with Christ (see

[2]M. Hengel, *The Pre-Christian Paul* (London: SCM, 1990; Philadelphia: Trinity Press International).

[3]H. Maccoby, *The Mythmaker: Paul and the Invention of Christianity* (New York: Harper & Row, 1986).

Phil 3:10) eventually led Jews to perceive Pauline Christianity to be a new religion. His liberal attitude toward Gentile converts to Pauline Christianity and his own willingness to share their lives (perhaps even to the point of not observing the Law, see 1 Cor 9:21) led Jewish Christians to suspect that Paul had gone over the edge of Judaism and of Jewish Christianity.

While consciously remaining within Judaism, Paul did engage at several points in what can be called a "redefinition" of Judaism that equated Jewish Christians and Gentile Christians with the remnant mentioned in the Jewish Scriptures. In Philippians 3:3, he redefines the circumcision as those "who worship in the Spirit of God and boast in Christ Jesus and have no confidence in the flesh." In Romans 2:13-16, he claims that Gentiles who "do instinctively what the Law requires" are a law to themselves and thus qualify as doers of the Law. In Romans 9:6, he redefines Israel to exclude some Jews: "For not all Israelites truly belong to Israel." And the basic issue that occupied Paul in his letters to the Galatians and Romans was how non-Jews could be part of the people of God, whose historic root remains in Israel (see Rom 11:17-24).

Paul never disavowed his Judaism. He never said: "I am no longer a Jew." In fact, at several points (Phil 3:5-6; 2 Cor 12:22; Rom 11:1), he lists his credentials as a Jew. But to say that Paul remained intensely proud of his Jewish credentials overlooks the contexts in which the lists appear. What Paul the Christian was most proud of was his participation in the death and resurrection of Christ. In the light of that experience, his Jewish credentials were at best indifferent and at worst "loss" (Phil 3:7-8).

Was Paul a convert? He probably viewed himself as moving from Pharisaic Judaism to Christian Judaism. Other Jews (and even Jewish Christians) viewed his move as more radical. His "easy" admission of Gentiles to the communities that he founded (they did not have to be circumcised or to observe the Law) and his liberal redefinitions of circumcision, Law-observance, and Israel seemed to other Jews as too drastic. They probably did view Paul as moving from one religion to another, or at least as moving beyond Judaism. Later Gentile Christians came to share their opinion that Christianity and Judaism are separate religions.

Apostle to the Gentiles

At several points in his letters (Rom 1:5; 11:13; 15:16, 18; 16:26; Gal 1:16; 2:2, 8–9), Paul emphasizes that God called him to preach the gospel to the Gentiles. He recognizes the outcome of the Jerusalem meeting described in Galatians 2:1-10 as a division of labor according to which he and Barnabas would minister to non-Jews and the other apostles would work with Jews. Since Paul never separated his gospel from its Jewish roots, in effect Paul was extending a form of Judaism to Gentiles and thus opening up to all the privileges granted to Israel.

Some scholars prefer to talk about the "call" of Paul rather than his "conversion."[4] Their point is that, rather than changing religions, Paul felt himself to have been called by God to a special mission: to bring the gospel of Jesus Christ to non-Jews and thus to integrate them into the people of God. At the same time, Paul insisted that these Gentiles did not have to undergo circumcision or take upon themselves all the obligations of the Torah. He regarded Jewish Christians who sought to impose these obligations on non-Jews as compromising the gospel. Though Paul may have looked upon circumcision and the "works of the Law" as matters of indifference, he was not indifferent to Gentiles taking up these practices. Paul understood his mission to the Gentiles as not entailing circumcision or Torah observance.

What has been said thus far in this section is important but not controversial. It is not controversial because it reflects what Paul himself said clearly. It is important because it provides the context for what Paul says in his letters, especially regarding Jews and Judaism. Paul directly addresses Gentile Christians and tries to help them locate themselves in God's people with reference to Jewish Christians and other Jews. The problems that he encounters are, for the most part, Gentile-Christian problems. We are not sure how Paul spoke to Jewish Christians (see 1 Cor 9:20: "To the Jews I became as a Jew, in order to win the Jews"). His ideal future had Jewish Christians and Gentile Christians united with the temporarily hardened part of Israel (Rom 11:25-26) in one people of God and all enjoying the benefits of salvation. In

[4]K. Stendahl, *Paul among Jews and Gentiles* (Philadelphia: Fortress, 1976).

reading Paul's letters, we must not lose sight of his Gentile-Christian audience.

Recognition that Paul preached primarily to non-Jews and that in his letters, he was almost everywhere (except in parts of Romans) addressing Gentile Christians is an important emphasis in modern Pauline scholarship. Two scholars—Francis Watson and Lloyd Gaston—have tried to develop these points in more depth and thus have arrived at two very different pictures of Paul as Apostle to the Gentiles. Though neither has found many followers, each argues his case with vigor and presents a surprisingly fresh picture of Paul.

Watson, in *Paul, Judaism and the Gentiles: A Sociological Approach* (Cambridge-London-New York: Cambridge University Press, 1986), seeks to explain Paul's attitudes toward Judaism, the Law, and Gentiles as part of his attempt to legitimate the social reality of sectarian Gentile-Christian communities in which the Law was not observed. According to Watson, when Paul wrote his letters, Gentile-Christian separation from the Jewish synagogues had already occurred. Moreover, Paul had already conducted an unsuccessful mission among Jews. That mission was so unsuccessful that Paul concluded that non-Christian Jews were subject to a divine "hardening," and that he was called to preach the gospel to Gentiles instead. The Gentile-Christian Churches founded by Paul constituted a sect outside the Jewish community, not a reform movement within it.

According to Watson, the separation of the Gentile Churches from the synagogue and from Judaism was the presupposition of Paul's letters to Gentile Christians. In the pertinent texts of Galatians and Philippians, Paul was arguing the case for viewing the Church as a sect outside Judaism. In Romans, one of Paul's goals was to persuade Jewish Christians to recognize the legitimacy of the Gentile-Christian congregation and to join with it in worship. This action, on the part of Jewish Christians, would inevitably mean a final separation for them also from the synagogue.

In Watson's perspective, Christian hope is independent of the Law and of Judaism, and Pauline Christianity is Gentile Christianity. Paul had already gone over the line from Judaism to Gentile Christianity, and he expected other Jewish Christians to follow, for there is only one kind of Christianity—Gentile Christianity. Watson regards "faith" and "works" as sociological markers or slogans for the ways of life practiced in the Pauline congregations and in the Jewish communities, respectively. The Law was not practiced in the Pauline congregations, and, therefore, the faith-works distinction was primarily sociological rather than theological. Since Paul's statements were so closely related to this unique and unrepeatable historical situation, their relevance for theology through the centuries and today is far more limited than has usually been recognized.

The dizzying effects of Watson's positions are matched on the other side by those of Lloyd Gaston in *Paul and the Torah* (Vancouver: University of British Columbia Press, 1987). Gaston takes very seriously the division of apostolic labor outlined in Galatians 2:7-9: Paul was the apostle sent to the Gentiles. He also takes very seriously that Paul, in his letters, wrote primarily, if not exclusively, to Gentile Christians. He also contends that Paul dealt with Gentile-Christian problems, "foremost among which was the right of Gentiles qua Gentiles, without adopting the Torah of Israel, to full citizenship in the people of God" (p. 23).

According to Gaston, Paul's experience of Christ on the road to Damascus had a specific content. It was that through Christ, God had provided a meaningful answer to the quandary concerning Gentiles and the Law. How were the Gentiles to be saved? That salvation was to take place "in Christ," for Christ was the fulfillment of God's promises concerning the Gentiles. Therefore, Jews do not need to become Gentiles, nor do Gentiles need to become Jews. Yet, both are full and equal members of God's people.

Since Paul was not addressing Jews or Jewish Christians, he had no intention of persuading them to abandon observance of the Torah. The implication is that Jews and Jewish Christians were to continue keeping the Torah. The result of this approach would seem to be two kinds of Christianity—one Jewish and one Gentile—something like the situation suggested by Galatians 2. Paul's quarrel with his fellow Jewish Christians was not their observance of the Law but rather, their failure to grasp what God was doing among the Gentiles through Christ.

Whereas for Watson the Pauline Churches had already split off from Judaism and constituted the mainline of Christianity, according to Gaston, throughout Paul's ministry, there remained two kinds of Christianity—one Law-observing (Jewish) and the other not Law-observing (Gentile). I regard both views as extreme and based on presuppositions that cannot be proved. Historical truth is probably somewhere in the middle: Paul wrote in the midst of the struggle over whether there really are two kinds of Christianity, and the logic of his position was that there is only one Christianity (whether his contemporaries or even Paul himself recognized it or not). But both Watson and Gaston show how different Paul looks when one takes seriously his call to be Apostle to the Gentiles.

Paul and the Law

When Paul used the Greek word *nomos*, he almost always meant the Mosaic Law, or the Torah. Indeed, it is a safe rule, in reading Paul's letters, to assume that *nomos* refers to the Law (with a capital L) unless there are reasons to think otherwise (see Rom 3:27; 7:21). Therefore, Paul's criticisms of the *nomos* are directed toward the Mosaic Law (at least the misunderstanding and misuse of it), not toward law in general.[5]

In writing to Gentile Christians, Paul made clear that willingness to observe the Mosaic Law was not a requirement for them. Since some of these Gentile Christians may have had some familiarity with Judaism and Jewish ways as associate members of synagogues ("God fearers" according to Acts), there may well have been the expectation in some quarters that Gentile converts to Christianity would undertake to observe the Jewish Law. Paul, however, insisted vigorously that Gentiles do not need to observe the Law.

Why was Paul so insistent on this point? The precise occasion for Paul's insistence escapes us now; see the discussion about "legalism" below. But Paul's basic theological reason is clear enough: Paul did not regard Christ and the Law as being on the same level. Only Christ could bring about right relationship with God (justification). Paul saw a danger that some people might

[5]For a good survey, see D. Moo, "Paul and the Law in the Last Ten Years," *Scottish Journal of Theology* 40 (1987) 287–307.

think that the Law could bring about right relationship with God. Perhaps he himself once thought that way. Therefore, Paul wanted to emphasize that the Law could not do what Christ did and does not belong on the same level.

In Paul's view, the Law must not be understood as a rival to Christ. That is a misuse or perversion of the Law. In its positive functions, the Law bears witness to Christ (Rom 3:21) and prepares the way for Christ as a guardian (Gal 3:24-25). In its negative functions, the Law served as an ally of sin and death by bringing knowledge of sin and thus enticing people to sin. The Law is secondary to Christ, both for Gentile Christians and Jewish Christians. Whether Jewish Christians (like Paul) fulfill it is a matter of secondary importance and one of indifference, though Paul was not indifferent to those who would force Gentile Christians to observe it.

Did Jews of Paul's time really believe that Torah observance could bring about right relationship with God (justification)? It is possible that some did. It is even possible that Paul once did (see Romans 7). But there is not much evidence for "legalism" within first-century Judaism. Most Jewish writings from the period place Torah observance in the theological context of God's election of Israel, gift of the Law, and ongoing relationship of covenant. Torah observance is typically the proper response to God's initiatives, not the means of securing and meriting God's favor.

This common pattern of Jewish piety has been called "covenantal nomism" by E. P. Sanders in *Paul and Palestinian Judaism* (Philadelphia: Fortress, 1977).[6] Sanders looked for the "legalism" that Paul battled, and he failed to find it anywhere in the writings of Second Temple Judaism. So, he suggested that Jewish "legalism" was more the product of Paul's theological reasoning than a living Jewish theological option in Paul's day. Paul's experience of Christ was so dramatic and powerful that Paul wished to put nothing else on the same level. Moreover, so liberating and life-giving was this experience that it solved Paul's personal and theological problems. He was already enjoying the benefits of being "conformed" to and participating in Christ.

[6]For a critique, see J. Neusner, "Comparing Judaisms," *History of Religions* 18 (1978) 177–91.

According to Sanders, much of what Paul said about Judaism and the Law derives from the peculiar logic of Paul's theology. He was reasoning from the solution (what happened to him through and in Christ) to the plight (what Christ freed him from). So, especially in Romans, Paul was reasoning backward from what wonderful things he regarded as now taking place for him (justification, access to God, forgiveness of sins, and so forth) to what terrible things he had been rescued from (the dominion of sin and death, the Law as their ally, and so forth). So as to emphasize the greatness of what Christ had done, Paul also emphasized the terrible plight in which humankind found itself before the coming of Christ (see Rom 5:12-21 for a powerful meditation on this theme).

Paul's primary theological interest was what God had done for humankind in Christ Jesus. The Law was at most a secondary interest, part of Paul's reasoning process from solution to plight. Therefore, we should not be surprised about the tensions (some say, inconsistencies or even contradictions) in Paul's statements about the Law.[7] In Galatians and Romans, Paul was writing primarily about the Christ-event and only secondarily about the Law. We should not be surprised if Paul was occasionally inconsistent regarding the place of the Law, since he was beginning the process of theological reflection on the topic.

Lloyd Gaston, in *Paul and the Torah* (p. 25), makes a fresh suggestion about Paul's struggle against "legalism." Since Paul was writing to Gentile Christians, then legalism was most likely a Gentile problem, not a Jewish problem. Whereas Jewish Christians could continue to live their lives in the traditional context of covenantal nomism, Gentile Christians, who were not "under the covenant," were at a loss as how to proceed. Some determined to do "the works of the Law" but were confused about what these were or should be in their case. Among such Gentile Christians, according to Gaston, the problem of "legalism" arose as they sought to build up their own kind of justification before God. Thus, legalism was not a Jewish aberration or a Pauline theological construct but rather, a Gentile-Christian invention that Paul sought to combat with his criticisms of those who undertake the "works of the Law."

[7]E. P. Sanders, *Paul, the Law, and the Jewish People* (Philadelphia: Fortress, 1985).

On the matter of Paul and the Law, Sanders' insights about Jewish covenantal nomism and Paul's reasoning from solution to plight are important contributions. However, it is not impossible that there were Jewish "legalists" who simply did not leave us a corpus of writings. Gaston's suggestion about Gentile legalists is ingenious but difficult to prove.

"Tensions" About the Law

Many of the perspectives on Paul's theology that Sanders developed are shared by the Finnish scholar, Heikki Räisänen. He, too, stresses that the starting point of Paul's thinking about the Torah is the Christ-event, not the Law. Since Paul was working backwards from the Christ-event to the Torah, the Law remained a theological problem for Paul, and Paul's theological attitude toward the Law vacillated. As Räisänen says in *Paul and the Law* (2nd ed.; Tübingen : Mohr-Siebeck, 1987): "Paul's most radical conclusions about the Law are thus strangely ambiguous." Therefore, Paul's handling of the Law is more of a theological problem for us than it is the solution of problems.

According to Räisänen, contradictions and tensions were constant features of Paul's theology of the Law. These "tensions" concern the Law's definition, validity, practicability, origin and purpose, and status.

Paul never defines what he means by Torah/*nomos*. He takes it for granted that his readers understand that it generally refers to the Mosaic Law. But even so, his use of the term oscillates wildly. At some points (Rom 2:14-15), it seems that non-Jews are subject to it and fulfill it. At other points (Rom 13:8-10), Paul appears to reduce the Law to love as the basic principle of the moral law. The liberating Christ-event is much clearer than the Law from which people are liberated.

Is the Law still valid? The "pedagogue" analogy in Galatians 3:23-26 indicates that the Law has been abolished: "But now that faith has come, we are no longer subject to a disciplinarian" (3:25). Likewise, the marriage analogy in Romans 7:1-6 suggests that Christians are no longer under the Law: "But now we are discharged from the Law, dead to that which held us captive . . ."

(7:6). On the other hand, in answer to the charge that Christians overthrow the Law, Paul answers: "By no means! On the contrary, we uphold the Law" (Rom 3:31). These different attitudes toward the validity of the Law meet in Paul's claim in Romans 10:4 that Christ is the *telos* of the Law: Is Christ the goal to which the Law pointed? Or is he its termination in the sense of its abolition? Or is he both?

Can the Law be fulfilled? Paul's description of how Jews needed the revelation of God's righteousness in Christ (Rom 2-3) denies that Jews kept the Law. Rather, they did what the Law forbade, and thus, the Law became for them a source of "the knowledge of sin" (3:20). All people—both Jews and Greeks—were thoroughly under the power of sin until the coming of Christ: "For no human being will be justified in his sight by deeds prescribed by the Law" (3:20). On the other hand, Paul declares that his own behavior with regard to the Law had been blameless: "as to righteousness under the Law, blameless" (Phil 3:6). Moreover, in the middle of his indictment of Jews for not observing the Law, Paul inserts the case of Gentiles who, though they do not possess the Law, "do instinctively what the Law requires" (2:14).

What were the Law's origin and purpose? Though Paul and his readers generally share the assumption that God gave the Law to Moses on Sinai, at one point (Gal 3:19-20) Paul suggests that God used mediators (angels) and that, therefore, the Law is inferior to the promise given directly to Abraham. At some points, the Law is an ally of sin and death. By fostering knowledge of sin (Rom 3:20), the Law gave life and power to sin: "Apart from the Law, sin lies dead" (Rom 7:8). The result of the alliance between sin and the Law is death: "For sin, seizing an opportunity in the commandment, deceived me and through it killed me" (7:11). On the other hand, Paul boldly states in Romans 7:12: "So the Law is holy, and the commandment is holy and just and good."

What is the status of the Law? As Räisänen says: "Paul implies that the Law is a rival principle of salvation, occupying in the Jewish system a place analogous to that of Christ in the new order of things." In his apocalyptic picture of reality, Paul placed the Law and its works along with sin, death, and flesh. These powers stand in opposition to Christ, the Spirit, grace, the promise, and faith. The great status and the negative role that Paul attributed to the Law are unique among Jewish and even early Christian writers not directly influenced by Paul. Why Paul ignored the theological framework in which Jews customarily placed the Law ("covenantal nomism") and why he so elevated the status of the Law (even if in a negative way) remain puzzling.

It is hard to know what to call these features of Pauline thought. What is the best word? Is it tensions, or confusions, or inconsistencies, or contradictions? What one calls them probably reflects one's prior positions on Paul as a thinker and on the nature of Scripture. Whatever one does call them, it is clear that on the matter of the Law, Paul's letters contain statements that appear inconsistent.

How are these tensions to be explained? The classical apologetic approach is to deny the presence of inconsistencies or contradictions in Scripture. But it takes a lot of ingenuity and special pleading to turn all the Pauline statements about the Law into a perfectly coherent position. Another classical mode of explanation is to appeal to the development of Paul's thought. For example, Hans Hübner[8] contends that in Galatians, Paul criticized the Law as such and taught that "Christ is the end of the Mosaic Law," whereas in Romans, Paul attacked the perversion of the Law and his message was "Christ is the end of the fleshly misuse of the Law." This approach has some merit. But it runs aground mainly because even within Romans itself, there are many tensions or inconsistencies regarding the Law.

One current solution is to give particular attention to the situation in which Paul wrote. This approach proceeds from the perspective that Paul wrote as a pastoral theologian trying to cast light on specific situations. In his directives, Paul necessarily used the language and slogans of opponents, or at least of the people whom he addressed. Moreover, Paul wrote not as a systematic theologian, but rather as a practical pastor. Therefore, we should not expect consistency from Paul on the Law, since his letters contain merely pragmatic responses to local pastoral problems.

---

[8]H. Hübner, *Law in Paul's Thought* (Edinburgh: T. & T. Clark, 1984).

Räisänen represents a fourth approach. According to him, Paul was still quite confused and ambiguous about the Law. And his confusion and ambiguity are reflected in what he said about the Law. This confusion had deep personal and historical roots. Therefore, it is a hopeless task to systematize what Paul said about the Law, or to plot the development of his thought on the Law, or to reconstruct the pastoral situations that Paul addresses.

There is probably some truth in all four approaches. Räisänen tends to find contradictions everywhere, sometimes even where most readers do not find them. It is likely, even in the short span of time in which Paul wrote his letters, that Paul's ideas on the Law did develop. This development may have been aided by the particular pastoral problems regarding the Law that Paul faced. And yet, when those first three explanations have been tried, there still remain some Pauline statements about the Law that resist attempts at defending their consistency and coherence. The insight that Paul was clearer about the solution (Christ) than about the precise nature of the plight is both valid and helpful in understanding Paul's statements about the Law.

Israel's Future

Whatever the precise details of Paul's position on the Law may be, one thing is clear: The Law cannot do what Christ does in bringing about right relationship with God. Therefore, in Paul's view, those who follow the Law rather than Christ are on the wrong path and exist in some kind of theological "limbo." According to the olive tree analogy in Romans 11:17-24, they are the branches broken off so that the Gentiles might be grafted in.

Though Paul described the present of non-Christian Jews in neutral or even negative terms, he nevertheless held out a future role for such Jews in the unfolding of God's mystery. That future role is outlined in Romans 11:25-26: "a hardening has come upon part of Israel, until the full number of Gentiles has come in. And so all Israel will be saved." The exegetical details and theological implications of this text have already been treated in chapter 4. Here, I wish only to take up the debate about a possible "separate way" to God for Israel.

In Romans 11:26a, Paul left unanswered three questions about Israel's future: Who? When? How? Who is the subject of the expression "all Israel?" In view of the argument developed by Paul and the logic of the sentence, "all Israel" seems to refer to "Israel" taken collectively—consisting of Jewish Christians and other Jews, not necessarily including each and every Israelite but surely enough to merit the title "Israel." When will the salvation of "all Israel" take place? It seems to be an eschatological event, one that will accompany the resurrection of the dead, the last judgment, and the full manifestation of God's kingdom. This eschatological event, of course, does not preclude Jews from becoming Christians in the present. But Paul probably envisioned not so much a long-term mission to the Jews as he did a sudden mass conversion on the part of "hardened" Israel as one aspect of the scenario of end-time events. And Paul expected this mass conversion to happen fairly soon (see Rom 13:11-12).

Though Paul is not explicit, one can be fairly certain about the first two questions: Who? All Israel is the collective of Christian and other Jews, along with the Gentiles who have "come in." When? At the end of human history, as part of the complex of eschatological events. The more difficult question is, How? There is one line of interpretation (the Christological) that takes Israel's eschatological salvation as necessarily connected with Christ. But there is another mode of interpretation (the theological) that contends that God has a separate way of salvation for "all Israel" apart from Christ.

The theological interpretation begins from the observation that from the end of Romans 10 and all through chapter 11, Paul does not mention "Christ" or "Jesus." He prefers to talk about "God." This approach, represented in various modes by John Gager, Lloyd Gaston, Franz Mussner, Krister Stendahl, and Paul van Buren,[9] argues that Israel's way of salvation is fidelity to the Torah. God will judge Israel on that criterion, not on the criterion of "faith" by which Gentile Christians (and presumably, Jewish Christians also) will be judged. This theological approach has great ecumenical potential because it allows Jews and Christians to view one another as partners along two different but equally effective

---

[9]See the list of suggested readings for the works of these scholars.

ways to God—the way of Torah and the way of Christ. In this perspective, there need be no special mission to the Jews on the Christian side, and Jews can rest secure that they and their children will not be the object of conversionary campaigns.

While the theological approach has some distinguished proponents and great ecumenical potential, it probably does not mirror what Paul thought. If we assume that Romans 9–11 is an integral part of the argument of Romans as a whole, and if we reflect on Paul's statements about Israel's need for the revelation of God's righteousness in Christ and about what Christ has done for all human beings (freed them from the dominion of sin, death, and the Law), it is very difficult to hold anything but the Christological interpretation of Romans 11:26a. The eschatological salvation of all Israel must have some explicit connection with the saving work of Christ. That, at least, is the logic of Romans.

Trying to identify the precise nature of all Israel's connection with Christ is even more difficult. Paul most likely assumed that, when he had preached the gospel to the ends of the earth (Spain?) and the full number of Gentiles had come in, Christ would come again as Deliverer (see Rom 11:26) and all Israel would be saved. And Paul probably expected that these events would occur in the near future.

Paul never hints at a second missionary campaign to Israel. That had already been done. The Jewish-Christian remnant had turned to Christ, and the other part of Israel remained hardened. The theme of the divinely induced jealousy at the conversion of the Gentiles (Rom 11:11, 14) suggests some stirring on the part of non-Christian Israel toward Christ. Its acceptance of the gospel, however, will mean "life from the dead" (Rom 11:15)—resurrection and the other eschatological events. Perhaps Paul hoped that "all Israel" would have the same kind of overpowering experience of Christ that he himself had.[10] In that sense, God does have a special way for Israel, and Paul's experience of Christ is its prototype or anticipation just as Christ's resurrection anticipates the resurrection of us all.

---

[10]O. Hofius, " 'All Israel Will Be Saved': Divine Salvation and Israel's Deliverance in Romans 9–11," *Princeton Seminary Bulletin* Supp. 1 (1990) 19–39.

6

Friend or Foe of Israel?

Is Paul the friend or the enemy of the Jewish people? Are Paul's writings the basis for a new and positive relationship between Christians and Jews, or a reason for a two-thousand-year history of hatred and suffering? Those questions, raised first in the introduction, come back to us now at the conclusion of this study. They are serious questions. But they cannot be answered satisfactorily with a simple yes or no.

To formulate a more adequate response, this chapter will first review briefly some of the main points that have emerged from this study of Paul on the mystery of Israel. Then, it will try to assess to what extent Paul is a friend of Israel and to what extent he is a foe of Israel. Finally, it will return to the point where the book began—Vatican II's statement on the Catholic Church's relationship with the Jewish people in *Nostra aetate* 4. There it considers what in Paul's letters can serve to found a new and more positive relationship between Christians and Jews, and what raises problems for that relationship.

Main Points

The first chapter, "Paul in Context," stressed the importance of taking Paul on his own terms. Paul wrote letters to various Christian communities as the extension of his apostolic activity in preaching the gospel and founding churches. His statements about Jews and Judaism are addressed to Gentile Christians and try to help them understand better their own new identity as Christians. Paul wrote as a Diaspora Jew, raised in a diverse and international kind of Judaism. He used the Greek language and rhetorical conventions of Greco-Roman authors to spread what he regarded as the "fullest" form of Judaism but what others considered apostasy from Judaism. Paul wrote as a pastoral theologian for whom the personal experience of Christ (see Phil 3:8-11) had been life-changing. He was concerned with community problems rather than individual ones. With regard to the mystery of Israel, he needed to explain how Gentiles could be regarded as part of God's people. The short time-span in which Paul's letters were written and their "occasional" character (responding mainly to the problems of others) make difficult any attempt to chart the development of Paul's thinking. On the mystery of Israel and every other topic in the New Testament, Paul said the "first word," and allowance must be made for his unique circumstances and his pioneering efforts.

The second chapter examined the Pauline texts on Jews and Judaism "Before Romans." It first set them in their historical context: Paul was addressing Gentile-Christian communities that he had founded. In Galatians, 2 Corinthians, and Philippians 3, there seems to have been pressure from Jewish-Christian missionaries for Gentile Christians to undergo circumcision and do the "works of the Law." Before discussing those very important texts, however, it was necessary first to look at 1 Thessalonians 2:14-16, only to raise questions about its importance: Was it part of the original text? If so, which Jews and how many are being criticized? Why does Paul resort to Jewish and pagan stereotypes?

The issue of the mystery of Israel appears first in Galatians. In Galatians 1–2, Paul defends not imposing circumcision on Gentile Christians by appealing to the divine origin of his own apostolic commission and to the Jerusalem apostles' approval of his gospel. He also resists the idea of separate Christianities (Jewish and Gentile) on the grounds that faith, rather than the Law, is the principle of right relationship with God. In Galatians 3–4, Paul confronts the issue of whether Gentile Christians need to observe the Mosaic Law. He argues that they do not need to do so on the basis of their personal experience (they already received the

Spirit without observing the Law) and by appealing to the Scriptures' presentation of God declaring Abraham "righteous" before the Law was given. The best that Paul can say about the Mosaic Law is that it helped people to recognize what sin is and served as a provisional guide ("pedagogue").

This opposition between the promise to Abraham that is fulfilled in Christ and the Mosaic Law is developed in 2 Corinthians 3. Paul there insists that Christ is the key to the Scriptures and that those who read them (Jews, and perhaps extremely conservative Jewish Christians) apart from Christ fail to understand them because their minds are veiled. Philippians 3 explains why Paul did not regard circumcision and Torah observance to be necessary for Gentile Christians and even for Jewish Christians like himself. His experience of being "conformed" to Christ convinced him that membership in God's people was available to all—Gentiles and Jews alike—and that the distinctive practices of Judaism were not important anymore.

The chapter on "Romans" first showed how Romans can be read both as a kind of theological synthesis and as practical advice on issues dividing the Christians at Rome. Then, it focused on Romans 2–3. There Paul argued that Jews, as well as Gentiles, needed the revelation of God's righteousness in Christ and that having the Law is no protection against God's wrath since the Law only brings knowledge of sin. The solution to the plight of both Jews and Gentiles is Christ, who frees all from the servitude of sin and death (and their ally, the Law) for life in the Spirit. Jews who continue to live by the Torah and imagine that it can do what Christ has done are on the wrong track according to Paul.

The mystery of Israel is the subject of Romans 9–11: Why has not all Israel accepted the revelation of God's righteousness in Christ? Paul recognized the election and continuing existence of Israel, and still viewed himself as part of it. He ascribed Israel's rejection of the gospel as somehow providential, by making room for Gentiles in God's people. Though non-Christian Jews are now on the wrong way (Torah) and should have heeded the gospel, God's fidelity and purpose guarantee that God can (and will) graft them back onto the "olive tree" that constitutes Israel in its fullness (Rom 11:23).

Chapter four dealt with the focal text for the theme "Paul on the Mystery of Israel": Romans 11:25-32. In it, Paul explained to Gentile Christians the "mystery of Israel": The present obduracy of part of Israel has been allowed by God so that the "full number" of Gentiles might come in, and so "all Israel" will be saved. The term "all Israel" is collective, including both Christian and non-Christian Jews. Its salvation seems to be eschatological—at the end of history as we know it. In the logic of Romans as a whole, there must be some connection with Christ.

The chapter on "Modern Scholarship" first argued that Paul regarded himself as a convert from one kind of Judaism (Pharisaic) to another (Christian). But other Jews (and perhaps Jewish Christians, too) viewed Paul as moving outside Judaism and, therefore, an apostate. Next, it stressed the importance of recognizing that Paul's audience was Gentile Christians and compared the very different approaches taken by Francis Watson and Lloyd Gaston to this fact. Then it showed why Paul insisted that Christ and the Law are not on the same level in bringing about right relationship with God, and raised the question of who the "legalists" were whom Paul was so intent on battling. Next, it examined Paul's various tensions (or inconsistencies, or contradictions) about the Law's definition, validity, practicability, origin and purpose, and status. Finally, it suggested that God's "special way" for the salvation of "all Israel" (Rom 11:25-26) must logically involve the person of Christ, and that Paul may have understood it as analogous to his own experience of Christ.

Friend and Foe

In light of the main points made in the body of this book, it is fair to conclude that Paul is both the friend and the foe of Israel.

That Paul regarded himself the friend and benefactor of Israel is clear. He brought to his letters all the abilities and skills that he developed in his education as a Diaspora Jew and a Pharisaic Jew. He regarded himself as bringing to non-Jews what God had accomplished through Jesus the Jew and looked forward to Jews and Gentiles worshipping the God of Israel together (see Rom

15:7-13). Even when criticizing Jews who refused the gospel, Paul retained the traditional conviction of Israel's preeminence in salvation history ("to the Jew first"). He admitted that Jews had been entrusted with the oracles of God (Rom 3:2). He remained convinced that the privileges granted to Israel ("the adoption, the glory, the covenants . . .," Rom 9:4-5) were "irrevocable" (Rom 11:29). His greatest personal disappointment was that not all Israel had accepted the gospel ("I have great sorrow and unceasing anguish," Rom 9:2).

Even though Paul was the apostle sent to the Gentiles (see Gal 2:7), he understood the Gentile churches to be in relation to Israel. The model for Gentile Christians was the Hebrew patriarch Abraham (Gal 3; Rom 4), whom God declared "righteous" before and, therefore, apart from the Mosaic Law. The Gentile Christians were grafted onto the olive tree, that is, Israel, according to Romans 11:17-24, with Jewish Christians providing the necessary continuity. At several points in Romans 11 (vv. 11, 14), Paul indicates that his mission to the Gentiles was really intended to bring about good things for non-Christian Israel, also. Gentile acceptance of the gospel would make Jews "jealous" and, therefore, eager to accept the gospel, too. If Jewish rejection of the gospel means riches for Gentiles, its acceptance by Jews will mean "life from the dead" (Rom 11:12, 15). And Paul holds out a glorious future for "all Israel" (even those who had not accepted the gospel), since God remains faithful to the promises to Israel (see 11:25-26; 9:6) and has not rejected the people (11:1). In these respects, Paul is the friend of Israel.

In other respects, however, it is easy to understand why non-Christian Israel might see Paul as a foe. Even if Paul thought that he was preaching a new form of Judaism rather than another religion, non-Christian Jews must have found that his claims about Christ and his indifference to the importance of Jewish institutions placed him outside the boundaries of traditional Judaism. Such Jews would have objected to Paul and other Jews living and eating in the same communities with Gentiles. They would have been put off by Paul's practice of redefining (so as to include Gentiles and exclude most Jews) such Jewish institutions as circumcision ("it is we who are the circumcision," Phil 3:3), as well as his claim that Gentiles do what the Law requires whereas Jews do not (Rom 2:12-16). And they would have been first confused and then enraged at Paul's redefinition of Israel itself to include Gentiles and exclude non-Christian Jews: "For not all Israelites truly belong to Israel, and not all of Abraham's children are his true descendants" (Rom 9:6-7).

Jews in Paul's time sometimes referred to circumcision as "the covenant," for to them, this rite meant the entrance of the Jewish male into God's covenant with Israel. And they looked upon the "works of the Law" as the appropriate response to God's election of Israel. Such people may well have been offended by Paul's negative comments about circumcision: "beware of those who mutilate the flesh" (Phil 3:2); "I wish those who unsettle you would castrate themselves" (Gal 5:12). They would have been puzzled and amazed at Paul's idea that the Mosaic Law was the ally of sin and death, and that one of its major functions was to increase consciousness of sin and thus sin itself (see Rom 3:20).

Though Paul never gave up on non-Christian Israel and held out a place for it in the glory of God's kingdom, what Paul says about non-Christian Jews in the present is not very flattering. Their minds are veiled, so that they do not properly understand their own Scriptures (2 Cor 3:15). They have been cut off from the life-giving olive tree and must await God's decision to graft them in again (Rom 11:23).

Paul and Nostra aetate 4

Are Paul's writings the basis for a new and positive relationship between Christians and Jews? Those who wrote section 4 in Vatican II's "Declaration on the Relationship of the Church to Non-Christian Religions" (*Nostra aetate*) certainly thought so. The first two-thirds of the section is really a paraphrase of the New Testament material in which Paul is "friendly" to Israel.

There is great emphasis on Abraham as the prototype of the Christian believer and acknowledgment that Christians are linked to the stock of Abraham. The conciliar text quotes Paul's list of Israel's privileges from Romans 9:4-5 and even adds a few to it. While admitting that most Jews did not accept the gospel and even opposed its spread (see Rom 11:28), the document cites Paul's opinion that the Jews remain dear to God, and that the gifts bestowed on them are irrevocable (Rom 11:29). It also appeals to Romans 11:11-32 for a hint about Israel's future and seems to suggest (cautiously) the eschatological interpretation ("the day, known to God alone").

This "Pauline" part of *Nostra aetate 4* represents an important theological perspective, for it affirms the Church's historical, organic connection with Israel. It thus roots ecclesiology in Israel as God's chosen people. The text also presents a remarkably positive picture of Israel: its status as beloved by God, its irrevocable privileges and its future unity with the Church.

There are, of course, some problems. The document leaves out all the "unfriendly" things that Paul said about Israel. Now, a conciliar document is not intended to be a biblical exegesis. And so, the writers had no obligation to include the negative side of Paul's view of the mystery of Israel. However, when one compares *Nostra aetate* 4 with Romans 9–11, one recognizes quickly that the biblical text offers a more complicated vision, and that the council's statement gives only one side of it.

Though the document labors mightily to emphasize the positive and to encourage a relationship of partners rather than enemies, it still contains some expressions, though dear to the Christian tradition, that reflect some of Paul's tendency to redefine Jewish institutions. I refer to such expressions as "the people of the New Covenant" and "the new people of God" to describe the Church. Such language is more at home in the "replacement" or "supersessionist" theologies represented by New Testament writers other than Paul. It suggests that the Church has taken Israel's place as God's people. On the other hand, the conciliar statement's description of Israel's future ("when all peoples will call on God with one voice and 'serve him shoulder to shoulder' ") is even vaguer than Romans 11:25-26 and, because of the context, less Christological than Paul was.

The final problem is that, on this matter, Romans 9–11 is a lonely voice in Paul's letters, and Paul's is a lonely voice within the New Testament. Only Paul gave much attention to the future of non-Christian Israel. And his statement in Romans 9–11 is full of redefinitions and (some say) confusions and contradictions. No other New Testament writer took up his lead and refined it in Paul's most characteristic directions: the Church's organic relation to Israel, God's continuing love for Israel, and its ultimate salvation. In this respect, Paul was a theological pioneer. Perhaps, as eschatological imminence cooled and the Church became more Gentile in orientation, it no longer seemed necessary to think about these matters.

As we look back on almost 2,000 years of Christian-Jewish relations, it is again important for us to think about the mystery of Israel as Paul did. The treatment in *Nostra aetate* 4 picked up from Paul some long forgotten perspectives and focused on the positive elements. To be fair, Christians and Jews must also look at the other, negative elements in Paul's exploration of the mystery of Israel, and try to understand the fullness of Paul's view. To do this is to respond to Vatican II's call for "biblical and theological enquiry" regarding the spiritual heritage common to Christians and Jews.

Appendix

The Text of *Nostra Aetate* 4

4. Sounding the depths of the mystery which is the Church, this sacred Council remembers the spiritual ties which link the people of the New Covenant to the stock of Abraham.

The Church of Christ acknowledges that in God's plan of salvation the beginning of her faith and election is to be found in the patriarchs, Moses and the prophets. She professes that all Christ's faithful, who as men of faith are sons of Abraham (cf. Gal 3:7), are included in the same patriarch's call and that the salvation of the Church is mystically prefigured in the exodus of God's chosen people from the land of bondage. On this account the Church cannot forget that she received the revelation of the Old Testament by way of that people with whom God in his inexpressible mercy established the ancient covenant. Nor can she forget that she draws nourishment from that good olive tree onto which the wild olive branches of the Gentiles have been grafted (cf. Rom. 11:17-24). The Church believes that Christ who is our peace has through his cross reconciled Jews and Gentiles and made them one in himself (cf. Eph 2:14-16).

Likewise, the Church keeps ever before her mind the words of the apostle Paul about his kinsmen: "they are Israelites, and to them belong the sonship, the glory, the covenants, the giving of the law, the worship, and the promises; to them belong the patriarchs, and of their race according to the flesh, is the Christ" (Rom. 9:4-5), the son of the virgin Mary. She is mindful, moreover, that the apostles, the pillars on which the Church stands, are of Jewish descent, as are many of those early disciples who proclaimed the Gospel of Christ to the world.

As holy Scripture testifies, Jerusalem did not recognize God's moment when it came (cf. Lk. 19:42). Jews for the most part did not accept the Gospel; on the contrary, many opposed the spreading of it (cf. Rom. 11:28). Even so, the apostle Paul maintains that the Jews remain very dear to God, for the sake of the patriarchs, since God does not take back the gifts he bestowed or the choice he made. Together with the prophets and that same apostle, the Church awaits the day, known to God alone, when all people will call on God with one voice and "serve him shoulder to shoulder" (Soph. 3:9; cf. Is. 66:23; Ps 65:4; Rom. 11:11-32).

Since Christians and Jews have such a common spiritual heritage, this sacred Council wishes to encourage and further mutual understanding and appreciation. This can be obtained, especially, by way of biblical and theological enquiry and through friendly discussions.

Even though the Jewish authorities and those who followed their lead pressed for the death of Christ (cf. John 19:6), neither all Jews indiscriminately at that time, nor Jews today, can be charged with the crimes committed during his passion. It is true that the Church is the new people of God, yet the Jews should not be spoken of as rejected or accursed as if this followed from holy Scripture. Consequently, all must take care, lest in catechizing or in preaching the Word of God, they teach anything which is not in accord with the truth of the Gospel message or the spirit of Christ.

Indeed, the Church reproves every form of persecution against whomsoever it may be directed. Remembering, then, her common heritage with the Jews and moved not by any political consideration, but solely by the religious motivation of Christian charity, she deplores all hatreds, persecutions, displays of antisemitism leveled at any time or from any source against the Jews.

The Church always held and continues to hold that Christ out of infinite love freely underwent suffering and death because of the sins of all men, so that all might attain salvation. It is the duty of the Church, therefore, in her preaching to proclaim the cross of Christ as the sign of God's universal love and the source of all grace.

Suggested Reading

(*especially recommended)

1. Paul and Judaism

Beker, J. C., *Paul's Apocalyptic Gospel. The Coming Triumph of God* (Philadelphia: Fortress, 1982).

_____, *Paul the Apostle. The Triumph of God in Life and Thought* (Philadelphia: Fortress, 1980).

Cunningham, P. A., *Jewish Apostle to the Gentiles. Paul as He Saw Himself* (Mystic, CT: Twenty-Third Publications, 1986).

Dahl, N. A., *Studies in Paul. Theology for the Early Christian Mission* (Minneapolis: Augsburg, 1977).

Davies, W. D., *Jewish and Pauline Studies* (Philadelphia: Fortress, 1984).

_____, *Paul and Rabbinic Judaism. Some Rabbinic Elements in Pauline Theology.* 4th ed. (Philadelphia: Fortress, 1980).

*Gaston, L., *Paul and the Torah* (Vancouver: University of British Columbia Press, 1987).

Hays, R. B., *Echoes of Scripture in the Letters of Paul* (New Haven-London: Yale University Press, 1989).

*Hengel, M., *The Pre-Christian Paul* (London: SCM, 1990; Philadelphia: Trinity Press International).

*Hübner, H., *Law in Paul's Thought* (Edinburgh: T. & T. Clark, 1984).

Lüdemann, G., *Opposition to Paul in Jewish Christianity* (Minneapolis: Fortress, 1989).

Maccoby, H., *The Mythmaker: Paul and the Invention of Christianity* (New York: Harper & Row, 1986).

Martin, B. L., *Christ and the Law in Paul* (Leiden-New York: Brill, 1989).

Meeks, W., *The First Urban Christians. The Social World of the Apostle Paul* (New Haven-London: Yale University Press, 1983).

*Räisänen, H., *Paul and the Law*. Rev. ed. (Tübingen: Mohr-Siebeck, 1987).

————, *The Torah and Christ* (Helsinki: Finnish Exegetical Society, 1986).

Richardson, P. and D. Granskou, eds., *Anti-Judaism in Early Christianity*. Vol. 1: *Paul and the Gospels* (Waterloo, Ont.: Wilfrid Laurier University Press, 1986).

*Sanders, E. P., *Paul and Palestinian Judaism. A Comparison of Patterns of Religion* (Philadelphia: Fortress, 1977).

————, *Paul, the Law, and the Jewish People* (Philadelphia: Fortress, 1985).

Schoeps, H. J., *Paul: The Theology of the Apostle in the Light of Jewish Religious History* (Philadelphia: Westminster, 1974).

*Segal, A. F., *Paul the Convert. The Apostolate and Apostasy of Saul the Pharisee* (New Haven-London: Yale University Press, 1990).

*Stendahl, K., *Paul Among Jews and Gentiles* (Philadelphia: Fortress, 1976).

Stockhausen, C. K., *Moses' Veil and the Glory of the New Covenant. The Exegetical Substructure of II Cor. 3, 1-4, 6* (Rome: Pontifical Biblical Institute, 1989).

Tomson, P. J., *Paul and the Jewish Law: Halakha in the Letters of the Apostle to the Gentiles* (Minneapolis: Fortress, 1990).

*Watson, F., *Paul, Judaism and the Gentiles. A Sociological Approach* (Cambridge, UK-London-New York: Cambridge University Press, 1986).

*Westerholm, S., *Israel's Law and the Church's Faith. Paul and His Recent Interpreters* (Grand Rapids: Eerdmans, 1988).

2. Romans

Badenas, R., *Christ the End of the Law: Romans 10:4 in Pauline Perspective* (Sheffield, UK: JSOT Press, 1985).

de Lorenzi, L., ed., *Die Israelfrage nach Röm 9-11* (Rome: St. Paul's Abbey, 1977).

*Donfried, K. P., ed., *The Romans Debate*. Rev. ed. (Peabody, MA: Hendrickson, 1991).

Dunn, J. D. G., *Romans 1-8; Romans 9-16* (Dallas: Word, 1988).

Elliott, N., *The Rhetoric of Romans. Argumentative Constraint and Strategy and Paul's Dialogue with Judaism* (Sheffield: JSOT Press, 1990).

Gorday, P., *Principles of Patristic Exegesis. Romans 9-11 in Origen, John Chrysostom, and Augustine* (New York-Toronto: Edwin Mellen, 1983).

Hübner, H., *Gottes Ich und Israel. Zum Schriftgebrauch des Paulus in Römer 9-11* (Göttingen: Vandenhoeck & Ruprecht, 1984).

Johnson, E. E., *The Function of Apocalyptic and Wisdom Traditions in Romans 9-11* (Atlanta: Scholars Press, 1989).

Kaylor, R. D., *Paul's Covenant Community: Jew and Gentile in Romans* (Atlanta: Knox, 1988).

Lübking, H. M., *Paulus und Israel im Römerbrief. Eine Untersuchung zu Römer 9-11*. (Frankfurt-Bern-New York: Peter Lang, 1986).

Migliore, D. L., ed., *The Church and Israel: Romans 9-11*. Princeton Seminary Bulletin, Supplementary Issue, No. 1 (Princeton: Princeton Theological Seminary, 1990).

Piper, J., *The Justification of God. An Exegetical and Theological Study of Romans 9:1-23* (Grand Rapids: Baker, 1983).

Refoulé, F., *". . . et ainsi tout Israël sera sauvé." Romains 11, 25-32* (Paris: Cerf, 1984).

Rhyne, C.T., *Faith Establishes the Law* (Chico, CA: Scholars Press, 1981).

Thielman, F., *From Plight to Solution. A Jewish Framework for Understanding Paul's View of the Law in Galatians and Romans* (Leiden-New York: Brill, 1989).

Wedderburn, A. J. M., *The Reasons for Romans* (Edinburgh: T. & T. Clark, 1988).

3. Christian-Jewish Relations

Barth, M., *The People of God* (Sheffield, UK: JSOT Press, 1983).

Callan, T., *Forgetting the Root. The Emergence of Christianity from Judaism* (New York-Mahwah, NJ: Paulist, 1986).

Gager, J. G., *The Origins of Anti-Semitism. Attitudes Toward Judaism in Pagan and Christian Antiquity* (New York-Oxford: Oxford University Press, 1983).

Harrington, D. J., *God's People in Christ. New Testament Perspectives on the Church and Judaism* (Philadelphia: Fortress, 1980).

Klein, C., *Anti-Judaism in Christian Theology* (Philadelphia: Fortress, 1979).

Koenig, J., *Jews and Christians in Dialogue* (Philadelphia: Fortress, 1979).

*Mussner, F., *Tractate on the Jews. The Significance of Judaism for Christian Faith* (Philadelphia: Fortress, 1984).

Sloyan, G. S., *Is Christ the End of the Law?* (Philadelphia: Westminster, 1978).

van Buren, P., *A Theology of the Jewish-Christian Reality*. 3 vols. (San Francisco: Harper & Row, 1980, 1983, 1988).

von der Osten-Sacken, P., *Christian-Jewish Dialogue. Theological Foundations* (Philadelphia: Fortress, 1986).

Williamson, C. M., *Has God Rejected His People? Anti-Judaism in the Christian Church* (Nashville: Abingdon, 1982).

Wilson, M. R., *Our Father Abraham. Jewish Roots of the Christian Faith* (Grand Rapids: Eerdmans, 1989).

Indexes

1. Principal Scripture Texts

2. Modern Scholars